CONTENTS

Chapter 1:
The giraffe and the freedom fighter

CLIVE HARBER, UNIVERSITY OF BIRMINGHAM
AND JEFF SERF, UNIVERSITY OF WOLVERHAMPTON

Introduction

"In 1978 I was working as a teacher in a college in Nigeria. At that time the British media was full of a story about a giraffe called Victor who had fallen over in a zoo and couldn't be helped to stand upright. At the same time Steve Biko, the South African black consciousness leader, was murdered in a South African jail. The Nigerian students were both mystified and horrified about the priorities of the British media. Living, working and researching in a foreign country was not only teaching me a lot about Nigeria but also about my own country." Clive Harber

Barely a week goes by without an article or advert appearing in the *Times Educational Supplement* encouraging international visits, links, exchanges and partnerships (physical and/or virtual) between schools, teachers and pupils. Such links take place for a whole series of reasons: so that teachers in Britain get to know more about the cultures of origin of their pupils, to make the national curriculum less euro-centric, to foster international understanding, awareness and respect, to encourage mutual learning but also, and importantly, to think about one's own society in the light of learning about another. All of these are good reasons to develop international links, but the challenge is to make such activities examples of quality global learning.

One danger of such links and visits is that they can turn into a form of educational tourism, where the participants visit educational institutions, meet fellow teachers and pupils and exchange experiences but where there is no real attempt to get beneath the surface, to try to understand the historical and political context of the countries and education systems concerned and, in the case of links with developing countries, does not try to set the experience in the context of theories of education and development.

This book's origins lie in a project which involved a group of UK teacher educators visiting South Africa and is based on an analysis of teaching and teacher education (using literature and evidence from student teachers in both the UK and South Africa) which suggests that teacher education does not, on the whole, provide student teachers with a political analysis of education, does not equip teachers to handle controversial political issues in the classroom and which does not use comparative or international examples to learn about the nature of education (Harber and Serf, 2007).

This was supported by a survey of teachers, pupils and teacher educators in the West Midlands in relation to education for global citizenship (Davies, Harber and Yamashita, 2005).

A recent article that discussed the experiences of forty PGCE initial teacher training students concluded that:

> "The training is overwhelmingly practical, concentrating on curriculum delivery and the ability to cope with a class ... And Theory? The reality is that the one-year course, whether university or school-based, barely scrapes the surface of what teachers ought to know. What about the history and politics of education? ... I asked (the students) to rate how important they thought an understanding of eight theoretical and policy issues was for a teacher. Then I asked how well their training helped them to understand each one. On most issues, a clear majority thought that teachers needed an understanding of the topic, but universities will be dismayed to see the low scores awarded for their teaching of it ... Deprived of a real understanding of both theory and policy, teachers are simply parroting the latest curriculum directives. Teachers in name, but technicians in reality." (Revell, 2005)

COURSE PREPARATION

The project entitled *Seeking Ubuntu: Education for Democratic Citizenship – Learning from South Africa* was a seven day study visit course carried out under the auspices of Teachers in Development Education (Tide~), a Birmingham based development education network. It stemmed from two earlier Tide~ projects, one of which aimed at comparing apartheid and post-apartheid education in South Africa with education in England to explore controversial issues in teacher education for democratic citizenship (Carter, Harber and Serf, 2003) and the other to use South Africa as a case study to explore key theories about the role of education in development (Harber and Serf, 2004). The project was a study visit course for nine teacher educators from Britain and Northern Ireland to Durban, South Africa. The aims for the course stated that:

> "The project will provide background on post-apartheid educational transformation, with a particular focus on teacher education. It will also provide participants with opportunities to explore some key issues often neglected in both schools and teacher education – conflict resolution and education for peace, masculinity, HIV/AIDS and the role of sport in education for democratic citizenship."

Among the specific aims were to:

- develop understanding of education and change in South Africa;
- engage in dialogue about post-apartheid reconciliation;
- provide a focus for debate about developments within education for citizenship in the UK;
- reflect on the implications for participants' own practice.

The course was designed to provide an academic context for analysing experiences during the visit and to confront important political issues within South African education as a basis for comparison with the UK.

The course began with a preparatory weekend in Birmingham. Beforehand participants were asked to read two books: George Alagiah's *A Passage to Africa* (2001) as an accessible discussion of post-colonial Africa, including South Africa, and a book on post-apartheid educational reform in South Africa (Harber, 2001). They were also asked to read a number of academic articles: Harber (2002) on education, democracy and poverty reduction in Africa in general; Enslin and Horsthemke (2004) on the relationship between ubuntu (a Zulu word for human dignity) and education for citizenship in African democracies, and Waghid (2004) on different concepts of citizenship education in South Africa.

The weekend began with a discussion of the group's reaction to this material and moved to a discussion of the nature of democracy and implications for education for democratic citizenship which was further informed by an extract from Carr and Hartnett (1996) which differentiates between deeper and more shallow forms of democracy. The paper by Harber and Serf (2007) referred to in the introduction was used to debate the nature of teacher education in Britain and South Africa and extracts from Carter, Harber and Serf (2003) were used as the basis for beginning a discussion of HIV/AIDS, masculinities and schooling and violence.

At this stage participants were asked to fill in an evaluation form that asked about what they had learned and how it might affect their practice. There was a general feeling that they had learned a great deal about Africa and the nature and purposes of South African education in particular. One participant put it that, *"It provided the social and political analysis to give a framework to what had previously been a jumble of ideas, knowledge and feelings".*

"Challenged my thinking about democratic citizenship and Britain's education system" was a common response. Given that this was a group of teacher educators with an existing interest in education for democratic citizenship, some of the individual responses were interesting:

"I will certainly address issues such as racism more directly."

"Particularly useful to think about education as a tool of stability within society – we do that to them because it is what we had done to us – I can see this in initial teacher training students' approach to teaching in the classroom."

"It has really made me think about how we (I) perpetuate the system."

"I will definitely reflect on schools as a violent institution – I can see it clearly now but I don't think I'd ever thought about it like that."

"It made me think about why we send children to schools."

"Masculinity/sexual violence was totally new to me."

THE COURSE IN SOUTH AFRICA

The week in Durban consisted of a combination of talks from academics and other speakers and visits relevant to the themes of the study visit. There were talks and discussions on current policy issues in South African education, the state of play in teacher education in South Africa, masculinity and education for democratic citizenship and the impact of HIV/AIDS on education in South Africa and Africa in general.

A whole day visit was organised to schools in the poor, rural Richmond area of KwaZulu Natal with a non-governmental organisation that had been working there on violence reduction. Richmond is an area that has been plagued with violence and gangsterism. In contrast, the group visited a well resourced, formerly white school in Durban as well as a black and Indian school in Durban that is involved in a project called *Dreams and Teams* about teaching democratic leadership and citizenship through sport, and which had involved a visit by British head teachers. Other visits included the KwaMuhle Museum of local history and a township tour.

At three points during the week the group discussed what for them had been the key points emerging from their experiences and then a final discussion of key issues on the last day.

KEY POINTS

- The clear sense of an overt democratic ideology permeating educational reform …

- … but also an awareness within educational policy that South Africa must survive in a competitive global economy;

- A sense of pride in the new South Africa;

- The ambitious nature of educational aims in South Africa;

- The gap between policy and the problems of implementation caused by staffing and other resources and the question of whether some of the policy was more 'symbolic' than real;

- The importance of teaching controversial issues both in schools and teacher education but …

- … the existence of silences and taboos on certain subjects;

- The question of 'who trains the trainers?' How do teacher educators learn to handle controversial issues and develop the confidence to do so?

- How can teacher education get to a stage where students (and tutors) 'live the course' i.e. where they experience democratic forms of learning and teaching as part of the course so that they are more likely to implement it in schools?

- Importance of principals and professional and committed teachers – material resources are not everything;

- The need for student teachers and pupils to have an understanding of the social structures shaping lives (race, class, gender etc) as well developing individual social skills in order to cope;

- The importance of considering men and masculinity in debates about gender and gender and violence;

- Is education always good for you? Does it actually harm some individuals and societies?

At the end of the week participants were asked to write a reflection on *What have you learned*:

about South Africa?

about the UK in the light of your South African experience?

about the role of teacher education in education for democratic citizenship?

about your professional practice in teacher education?

Also:

How might the preparatory weekend and this week influence your professional practice on your return to the UK?

If you've undertaken any study visit or link visit to South Africa or elsewhere, how was this different?

What have you learned about yourself?

In response to the first question participants commented on their own lack of knowledge prior to the visit and how the visit facilitated comparative study. One noted,

> "This visit allowed me the opportunity to delve much more deeply into the education system and gain a more informed body of knowledge about how things really are. In particular I began (almost without trying) to place what I saw in a comparative context with Northern Ireland, which like South Africa would be considered a 'beleaguered nation.'"

She then went on to discuss the many parallels between the experience of the two places. Another participant, who had previously visited the Eastern Cape Province, noted that:

> "I have a much deeper understanding of the diversity of South Africa. It has made me realise the complexities of the society and made me feel that I know even less about South Africa than before I came because I'm sure that if I went to Cape Town or Kimberley I would get yet another South Africa."

Others commented on the importance of the South African Constitution in educational thinking, the sense of vision and optimism in South Africa, the overwhelming impact of HIV/AIDS and overall one participant commented that **"we have a great deal to learn from South Africa".**

This point was continued in relation to the second question: What have you learned about the UK in the light of your South African experience? One theme that emerged was that the UK lacked the same sense of shared vision based on a common set of democratic values that the group sensed in South Africa. One participant noted, *"The UK could certainly learn from things that are happening in South Africa. We need a clearer philosophy/vision for the country. Where are we going? What are our true values? ... Democracy is taught through citizenship – it should be embedded in all we do."*

Others said, *"I'm fascinated and inspired by the clear vision of the purpose of education in South Africa and its links to the constitution and this has highlighted for me the lack of clarity in our own aims in the UK"* and *"I envy the constitution ... the sense of direction ... many of our central government policies seem disjointed and founded upon political expediency."* One participant commented that *"an earthquake event such as South Africa 1994 might be useful in giving focus for where we are going in education ... the lack of clear aims and values (lack of a constitution) leads to a muddled lack of focus feeling to our system."*

Another theme was that in the UK we rely too heavily on material resources and that we should be able to achieve far more, given all the resources in the UK system: *"... resources are often seen as a reason for not doing something. The visits we have been on show what can be done with very limited resources."* Another participant said, *"Having the latest computer, Interactive Whiteboard etc doesn't make you a great teacher."*

Finally, one participant observed that, *"We avoid controversy – I already knew that but it has been strengthened for me"* and interestingly added, *"It is/may be very difficult to be a true dissenter in both countries."*

The third question asked what they had learned about the role of teacher education in education for democratic citizenship. One participant commented, *"Teacher education is imperative if we genuinely wish to create education for democratic citizenship. Many teachers in Northern Ireland have not bought into this and are more concerned with examination results ... Many children and teachers are bored by citizenship education because they don't really see education as much more that a process to gain credit to move on to a different phase."*

The course seems to have widened the participants' perspective on citizenship education and the implications for teacher education. One participant talked of it *"not being just another curriculum area, it is a way of being – it requires a seismic shift in outlook and practice."* One noted that, *"So many trainees seem to have the model of a teacher as someone who spouts knowledge from the front"*, while another argued that the role of teacher education should not be to replicate prior education, but to create new educational opportunities and that this should involve alternative methods to those now practised but, as another said, *"since the curriculum is so prescriptive, we need to be mavericks in the system to make a difference."* Another participant, who is responsible for staff development in citizenship in a local authority, commented that she had learned the need for a whole school approach: *"I would like to shift my focus from working with and facilitating citizenship teachers in my LEA to working with those responsible for citizenship in each school on whole school training. In addition the importance of the buy in from senior management and the embedding of citizenship in the School at a structural and policy level has been highlighted and I would like to shift my focus to that in the future".*

One participant in particular captured the overall conclusion from the course:

> *"We should be making trainees more aware of their role within education for democratic citizenship and looking at education's role more holistically rather than accepting our current model. There should be more time spent on comparing contrasting approaches and critically examining them. Trainees and ITT providers should also be asking the bigger questions which we have been tackling through the study visit: what is the role of education? How do we/can we provide education for democratic citizenship? What is democratic citizenship and how are we modelling it within ITT, within schools and within classrooms?"*

This question was followed by two on their own professional practice in teacher education. One common response was to use comparative South African material in their teaching but, as the following responses demonstrate, a key overall theme was the need to practice what is preached – to actually work in a more democratic way with student teachers in teacher education in order to prepare them for education for democratic citizenship in the classroom.

> *"I need to model democratic citizenship further in my own work with colleagues – the course has challenged me to seek ways of working more democratically with trainees."*

> *"I would like to work more on developing a democratic approach to elements of the PGCE programme ... I hope that something is developed so that the student teachers might be encouraged to use more democratic approaches in classroom placements."*

> *"I will consider passing more ownership to students."*

> *"I need to do more on masculinity with trainees and the importance of emotional literacy."*

> *"We need more democracy in practice in our scheme of work rather than delivering to students 'second hand'."*

> *"I need to encourage trainees to be critical thinkers and to help them to realise there are opportunities to be subversive."*

This theme reflects the argument that if schools are to be structured and operate in a more democratic way, then teachers need to learn ways of working democratically in both the whole school and the classroom as an integral part of their teacher education, given that their previous experience in school and higher education will not necessarily have prepared them.

However, teacher education has been characterised by the 'myth of the liberal college' – that is the myth that there is a contradiction between the liberal, progressive and democratic college or university on the one hand and the traditional, conservative and authoritarian school on the other. (The nature and origins of the predominantly authoritarian structure of formal schooling globally is discussed in more detail in Harber, 2004: ch.2). This myth suggests that student teachers are exposed to the more radical, democratic forms of teaching and learning during their courses in higher education but are rapidly re-socialised into more authoritarian understandings and practices during their teaching practice and their subsequent employment in education. Rather than there being a contradiction between the two, in terms of power over what is taught and learned, how, and when, let alone the contradiction between 'do as I say and do as I do' – it is argued that teacher education is often an authoritarian preparation for teaching in schools (Harber, 1994; Harber, 1997: ch.4). Moreover, it can also be argued that education for democratic citizenship needs to employ a critical social and political perspective examining the nature of the social structures that shape our lives, for example, the economy, 'race', gender and power structures.

The group were also asked if they had undertaken any work related or link visits before and how, if at all, this visit was different. They commented, for example, on:

- the mixture of academic sessions and practical activities such as visits to schools;
- the shared preparation and follow-up;
- being supported by experienced academics.

One participant said that she had been on a similar study visit to North America and that, *"It took me several months to digest what I had learned and reflect on it but it did make a major difference to my practice and to the ethos of my school."* However, it did not specifically require her to do the comparative exercise in the way that this study visit had and that this had been very valuable, helping her to think more analytically.

Finally, the participants were asked how the visit affected them personally. Some of the responses were a little surprising given that the participants were all experienced teachers and teacher educators.

> *"I have regained some self-confidence."*

> *"My values are shared by those in other networks and settings."*

> *"I've learned that there are others who feel like I do in terms of lack of confidence in our abilities."*

> *"It has confirmed that there are others who take a different slant on what can be learned."*

> *"I know a lot less than I thought I did (from a participant who had already visited and taught in South Africa)."*

> *"The effective/emotional has been at least as important as the "theoretical/academic."*

> *"That I accept and am excited by the fact that I have so much to learn and that my enthusiasm is shared by others."*

This highlights the importance of a comparative approach but also a certain amount of isolation of those working in teacher education and the need for a stronger network for those wishing to take a more comparative and critical approach to teacher education.

INTERVIEWS: ONE YEAR ON

A year after the study visit, in the summer of 2006, interviews were carried out with six of the group members to discuss if and how the visit had affected them as educationalists and how it had affected their professional practice.

In terms of how it had affected them, all group members commented on how *"looking beyond the tourist veneer"* had changed their perceptions and perspectives on education, even using words like *"inspired"* and *"profound learning experience"*. Two commented on how they had experience of other educationalists who had been on study visits where the main purpose was to 'help them' or 'advise them' (i.e. the teachers of the country visited) whereas it was just as important or more important to learn from other countries, compare and use the experience to evaluate one's own country. Two said that the comparative experience changed the way they looked at education. One said, for example, that it made her *"realise how little we actually question why we do things in education – what is education for? Why do we do it like this?"* Another commented on the collaborative and cooperative focus of the study visit, something that isn't always easy to achieve in the often individualistic and competitive ethos of higher education. Another said that the study visit had had a significant impact upon his confidence as a professional. The travel and group work with colleagues from other institutions had shown him how his contribution could be valued and this had helped his confidence in his own institution.

In terms of the impact on professional practice, there seems to have been some very practical and concrete outcomes. One group member had followed up on the study visit session on leadership and citizenship through sport and had attended a meeting in London where she met with the Youth Sport Trust, the British Council and some of the head teachers who had gone to South Africa as part of the original *Dreams and Teams* project. On the day we interviewed her she had been at a meeting linking 12 sports colleges in the Birmingham area which involves joint head teacher training, staff training and student exchanges between these schools and schools in South Africa. The key theme of this project is to be sport as a vehicle for leadership and citizenship. This was her initiative and was a direct outcome of the study visit. Another member of the group had been asked to make contributions to both a B.A. and M.A. course at her institution based on the study visit, with a specific focus on misconceptions of Africa. She had always done a session on teaching controversial issues as part of her PGCE teaching but now focused this specifically on HIV/AIDS because of the visit. She felt that the study visit had given her higher status within her institution: *"People are more aware of you"*. Another member of the team mentioned how she used comparative ideas from the study visit in interviewing new PGCE students and as part of the 'Student Associate Scheme' which is where potential students get a taster course before deciding whether to apply for a full teacher education course. She also runs a Diversity Group for non-white students at the University where she works and her South African experience has fed into this as well as trying to encourage all trainees to think more globally, though she acknowledged that problems of time, space and the inevitable for 'tips for teachers' made asking and discussing more fundamental questions about education more difficult.

Another group member had introduced a new module called *Beyond the Curriculum Boundaries* as a result of the study visit, which looked at questions of why we educate from a comparative perspective and has introduced sessions on teaching controversial issues because he felt that this wasn't receiving sufficient attention in the college. As a result he led a workshop on education for global citizenship for other teacher educators, where he and students who had studied this module discussed the principles behind the module and the content and shared their work with the other workshop participants. He took some students from his college to a conference called *Beyond Clause 28* and had taken part in a TV programme on homophobic bullying.

He also tackled both bullying and homophobic bullying in classes at the college. The Ubuntu study visit had made him ask *"who is doing this in our teacher education courses?"* and had both provoked this questioning and given him the confidence to act on these issues. As a result of the confidence that the study visit had given him he provided a consultancy for a college in Rio de Janeiro and used the opportunity to visit primary schools in rural Paraguay – he described this as a 'domino effect' stemming from the South Africa visit. Another group member described the visit as *"life changing ... one of the most interesting weeks of my life".* She felt her brain was 'addled' because it had had so much stimulation because of looking at the issues from different angles – she felt stretched intellectually. In terms of how the project had affected her professional practice, she had included a short unit of work in a Key Stage 3 (Year 9) class at the upper secondary school she worked at part-time in addition to her part-time post at the University. She now used South Africa as a comparative case study to help student teachers look outside their own system and use alternatives to critique the status quo. She also presented a paper with two other group members at a teacher education conference, the first time she had done this and, although 'petrified', felt that both the course and the paper had boosted her confidence. Finally, the last member to be interviewed noted that as a result of the visit she volunteered to teach on a new undergraduate course on international development and was going to apply for a role in a project on the global dimension in teacher education. She felt altogether more comfortable tackling controversial issues with students and a role play that she had been doing on apartheid for some time with students could now at last be updated to the post-1994 period.

CONCLUSION

This book stems, then, from the experience of the study visit to South Africa. Group members opted to use the experience to reflect on what they regarded as key aspects of education for democratic citizenship and their implications for teacher education.

Some chapters, such as those by Linda Clarke and Karen Teasdale, examine educational change in South Africa and draw out lessons for the UK while the chapter by Jackie Lambe is an overtly comparative study of inclusive education in two locations with many similarities in their histories. Some chapters (Helen Miles, Jenny Hughes and Liz Bartley) focus on curricular issues and citizenship – physical education, music, citizenship education itself. Other contributors examine significant and controversial issues affecting education – masculinity (Richard Woolley), HIV/AIDS (Sue Bermingham) and sustainability (Doreen Oakley).

A final chapter by the two editors looks at the attitudes and experience of student teachers themselves in both England and South Africa in relation to both democracy and the role of schools in education for democracy.

This evidence suggests that the contributors are right to be concerned about both the issues they write about and the contribution of teacher education to education for democratic citizenship, as schooling presently seems some way removed from making a full contribution to the development and maintenance of a democratic society and an awareness of that in its global context.

KEY POINTS

- There is a wide range of different types of international links between educators, learners and educational institutions.

- Without considering the historical, social, cultural, economic and political contexts, one can only gain a partial understanding of educational policies and practices.

- Structured group discussion enables learners to reflect on their experiences and consolidate their understanding.

- Learners respond to challenge if they perceive that they are supported and respected.

- Democratic practices are not incompatible with teacher education – in fact, they are essential if educators are to provide learners with the necessary knowledge, skills and experiences so they can become citizens in a democratic society.

REFERENCES

Alagiah, G. (2001) *A Passage to Africa.* London: Time Warner.

Carr, W. and Hartnett, A. (1996) *Education and the Struggle for Democracy: The politics of educational ideas*. Buckingham: Open University Press.

Carter, C., Harber, C and Serf, J. (2003) *Towards Ubuntu: Critical Teacher Education and Citizenship in South Africa and England.* Birmingham: Development Education Centre.

Davies, L., Harber, C. and Yamashita, H. (2005) *Global Citizenship Education: The Needs of Teachers and Learners*. University of Birmingham: Centre for International Education and Research.

Enslin, P. and Horsthemke, K. (2004) Can Ubuntu Provide a Model for Citizenship Education in African Democracies? *Comparative Education*, 40 (4), pp545-558.

Harber, C. (1994) International Political Development and Democratic Teacher Education. *Educational Review*, 46 (2), pp159-66.

Harber, C. (1997) *Education, Democracy and Political Development in Africa.* Brighton: Sussex Academic Press.

Harber, C. (2001) *State of Transition: Post-Apartheid Educational Reform in South Africa.* Oxford: Symposium Books.

Harber, C. (2002) Education, Democracy and Poverty Reduction in Africa. *Comparative Education*, 38 (3), pp267-76.

Harber, C. (2004) *Schooling As Violence: How Schools Harm Pupils and Societies.* London: RoutledgeFalmer.

Harber, C. and Serf, J. (2004) *Exploring Ubuntu: Education and Development, An Introduction to Theories and Debates.* Birmingham: Development Education Centre.

Harber, C. and Serf, J. (2007) Teacher Education for a Democratic Society, *Teaching and Teacher Education*, 22 (8), forthcoming.

Revell, P. (2005) Professionals or Parrots? *Education Guardian* 8/3.

Waghid, Y. (2004) Compassion, Citizenship and education in South Africa: An opportunity for Transformation? *International Review of Education*, 50 (5-6), pp525-542.

CHAPTER 2:

VOICES FROM SOUTH AFRICAN EDUCATION:

'TREAT THOSE TWO IMPOSTORS JUST THE SAME'

LINDA CLARKE, LECTURER IN EDUCATION, UNIVERSITY OF ULSTER

INTRODUCTION

This chapter is based around taped interviews with a convenience sample consisting of six Educators (Ed), two Student Teachers (ST) and seven Head Teachers (HT) who were each asked to cite the advantages and disadvantages of the current South African education system. The interviews were transcribed. What emerged amongst these *"Voices from South African Education"* was a startling degree of unanimity around two key issues. A strong admiration for government policy (in the form of the 1994 Constitution and in more recent central government legislation) seemed to be matched by an equally strong dissatisfaction about the implementation of policy.

The first finding seems startling to UK-based teachers, the majority of whom are unlikely to either cite or praise government policy. The disappointment with implementation, however, has undoubted resonance within the UK as is shown in the results of the *General Teaching Council's (England) Survey of Teachers* (NFER, 2005). The author suggests that it is professionally healthy for educators to, with apologies to Kipling, *'treat those two impostors just the same'* – to engage in the creative questioning of both policy and implementation whether these are deemed worthy of admiration or derision. These interviews have strengthened my resolve to ensure that student teachers start to develop the professional autonomy which will ensure that they are prepared to make their voices heard in discussions that inform both policy and practice.

This 'research' is, of necessity, somewhat reductionist and no claims are made for methodological validity. The tiny sample was based on opportunity alone. However, the unanimity of the responses and the intimate insights which are provided, resonate clearly with the seminal work of Fiske and Ladd (2004).

This chapter will report on these interviews in two ways. Firstly, the study will use the analytical lens provided by Fiske and Ladd's (2004) summary of the three key insights which they gained from their study of education in post-apartheid South Africa. Secondly, they will be used as a springboard for a brief discussion of *creative mediation* (Pollard, 2002:22), the questioning and subversion which should be part of the professional education of teachers throughout the world.

Elusive equity

Fiske and Ladd (2004) set out to explore the reasons why the educational equity that was espoused so clearly in the new South African Constitution has, thus far, proved to be so disappointingly elusive. They conclude with three inter-connected insights: **history matters**, **resources matter** and **implementation matters**.

History matters

The legacy of apartheid has left South Africa with a grossly uneven playing field which continues to affect possibilities for play on that field. History has both positive and negative impacts. The former exist because Nelson Mandela and other influential South Africans were willing to put past evils behind them as they shaped the Constitution. To the eyes of an outsider a clear example of a visionary pragmatism is exemplified by the decision to retain the elite schools like the one we visited in central Durban. Here, during the apartheid regime, in an environment which resembled Roedean, only wealthy white girls were taught and both fees and academic standards were high. It would have been easy for the post-apartheid government to close such schools. Instead they were retained and the new government insisted that they welcome learners of all races. Nonetheless, the fees for such schools are still relatively high and they attract only the wealthy urban elite, but all races are represented amongst the pupils and staff. On visiting the school, we witnessed the segregation of race which is immediately apparent in the playground where students of different races socialise separately over their packed lunches. Such negative impacts of history are perhaps readily identified.

Elements of racism and racial tension, of massive financial inequity and antagonism still permeate South African society. Such differences have influenced how far and how fast national policies can be implemented. Fiske and Ladd (2004) note, too, that various residues of the struggle against apartheid mean that it continues to be difficult to ensure adequate quality control and accountability. Popular resentment of authoritarian regimes led to the rapid introduction of Outcomes-based Education (OBE) in *Curriculum 2005* without a full consideration of its appropriateness for South Africa. The government also has to value the ways in which teachers and their pupils were partly responsible for the dismantling of apartheid. However, teachers must combine professional accountability with an autonomous and critical role that informs a healthy democracy, as suggested by Freire (1998:41)

> "To the extent that I become clearer about my choices and my dreams which are substantively political and attributively pedagogical, and to the extent that I recognise that though an educator I am also a political agent, I can better understand why I fear and realise how far we still have to go to improve our democracy. I also understand that as we put into practice an education that critically provokes a learner's consciousness, we are necessarily working against myths that deform us. As we confront such myths, we also face the dominant power because those myths are nothing but the expression of this power."

The impact of history comes across both positively and negatively in the interviews.

> "I think at the moment that one of our strengths is that we are living in an environment that is changing so completely that the education is able to change ... the opportunity to improve in a systemic way rather than piecemeal ways that often happen in other countries." (Ed1)

> "I think that one of the problems that has happened in America and the UK is that the environment is static, that the education system is static." (Ed1)

The interviewees' comments about the constitution and policy sounded, to an astonished UK academic, like something akin to outright adulation, although some were less emphatic.

> "So I think they are making every attempt to make sure that all children of South Africa get a holistic education, and that is a wonderful thing because previously many children couldn't go to school because it was too expensive, because it was far away from home, because school fees were different for people of different races." (HT1)

> "I think one of the other strengths we've got … as South Africa begins to move more globally and we begin to see ourselves more part of the global community … that education is beginning to shift into providing education with job creation. I think there's great interest now in terms of maths and science, it's about preparing kids for a global community in terms of jobs. I certainly think South African children are going to be able to perform in a global environment quite well. When you talk to, some British kids or American kids, a lot of our kids are really quite well educated. They've got a political understanding, they've got community understanding … there is a broader education …" (Ed1)

> "The strength of the South African education system, I think, is the clarity of purpose. That is the great strength. As we've said … there is a clear ideology, a clear philosophy which has then been articulated, it's been spelt out what the implications of that are right across the curriculum and it's reflected in the curriculum document, the management document." (Ed4)

> "We look great on paper." (Ed1)

It was surprising that not all made reference to racism. The white Head Teacher perceived there to be a problem with the way in which whites are perceived in the new South Africa:

> "One of the things that is really difficult to work through in our new democracy is that those of us who are white … it is not perceived that we have bought in to the new South Africa and that makes it really difficult." (HT5)

Racism was mentioned by both of the student teachers (both Asian) one of whom suggested that it had diminished and the other suggested that it was still a problem, with the latter adding that affirmative action (measures designed to redress inequality) was an even bigger problem.

RESOURCES MATTER

Fiske and Ladd (2004) suggest that South Africa's post apartheid educational reforms were driven largely by 'an equity imperative'. They detail the various mechanisms by which the government has sought to bring about a fairer distribution of educational resources across this vast country (at 1,219,912 sq km the area of South Africa is c. five times that of the UK). There have been some successes in equal treatment, in particular, the creating of an inherently race-blind system. However, the county has been less successful in providing the equality of opportunity which exists in principle but not in reality.

In terms of educational adequacy, Fiske and Ladd (2004) suggest that South Africa has made little progress with repetition and drop out rates still very high among black students. Furthermore, whilst South Africa did succeed in redistributing some resources from rich to poor provinces, this is not sufficient to lead to equity as was made clear in a South African *Sunday Times'* report which we read upon taking off from Durban:

> "At present, 3.6 million children do not have a chair to sit on, and 4.2 million do not have proper surfaces to write on."
> (Sunday Times Aug 14th 2005 on R12-billion rescue plan for schools)

As we travelled around the impoverished schools in Richmond my question about disadvantages of the education system seemed to be increasingly crass and unwarranted. Certainly, as far as resources were concerned there seemed to be few possible advantages and innumerable problems. Only two of the educators cited resource advantages, referring to improvements in funding in HIV/AIDS education (certainly every classroom we visited had vivid and candid posters about this) and for teacher training. These comments were each refuted by the interrelated comments of two others who cited the HIV/AIDS-related illness and death of trained and trainee teachers as major problem. The additional funding for teacher education, however, may be, as is the case in many less economically developed countries, providing trained teachers for richer countries. The (teacher) educator who mentioned this was referring, very pointedly, to the UK:

> *"We are not training teachers for ourselves; we are training them for a very rich country who should be training their own teachers."* (Ed3)

This pattern is confirmed by a recent BBC Online report which (http://news.bbc.co.uk/1/hi/world/africa/3629657.stm - accessed 15th Feb 2006) quoted Professor Kader Asmal, South African Minister for Education who suggested that *"at any one stage, up to 5,000 South Africans are teaching in London alone. "*

Poverty and poverty-related issues were mentioned by all respondents including the Head Teacher of a well-resourced, ex-White school in Durban, who was interviewed in her gracious and spacious study. She was fully aware of the problem:

> *"... it would seem to me, and this is a personal opinion, that there is no narrowing of the gap. If anything is happening, the gap is widening and I think that is true probably in many areas in life; the rich are getting richer, the poor are getting poorer, good schools are getting better and poor schools are getting worse. There are exceptions to that but I think the real challenge is to try and bridge the gap without diluting the standards and the good work that has been done in certain areas. I'm not just talking about the good work that has been done in the schools like this. I am talking about this good work that has been done in rural areas, but it is just not enough and I don't know if it's ever going to be enough."*

The poignant hopelessness of the final words of this quote echo Fiske and Ladd's (2004) ultimate conclusion:

> *"Equal treatment is not sufficient as a guiding principal of equity."*

There were indications too that resources were not being fully utilised. One comment had resonance with the introduction of computers in UK schools:

> *"What we see when we visit rural schools is they lock the library up because they're precious and so books are seen as something you must look after, not as something you must use."* (Ed1)

IMPLEMENTATION MATTERS

Fiske and Ladd (2004) note that South Africa indisputably has a number of well designed policies on the books now, but what has been lacking, in many cases, has been the capacity to implement these programmes in an efficient, non-corrupt, and effective manner.

All of the interviewees cited problems of implementation. The most commonly mentioned problems concerned managerial systems, leadership and the pace of change, which was seen to be both too ambitious and too experimental:

> "The weakness is the manifest inability of many of the managerial systems to deliver on the promise and the almost idealistic envisioning of some of the transformational moves that have taken place … and it actually may compound many of the problems that were inherited because too much is being attempted in too short a time." (Ed2)

> "In practice, it has been 11 years and a huge amount has happened but perhaps too much has happened. Our education ministers, for example, have been on something of a crusade to introduce all sorts of new innovations and to a large extent we have an anonymous situation in which the national department of education generates policy after policy after policy without due regard to the capacity of the provinces who are responsible to implement those policies or indeed to finance them." (Ed6)

In the face of a plethora of government policies the nature and provision of continuing professional development was cited by all of the Head Teachers:

> "The other weakness is sometimes when a new system or new methodology is implemented, training is insufficient, and we are not given enough time to sort of implement it and improve on it …" (HT1)

> "There is a problem of actual professional behaviour, a culture of professionals, which isn't fully formed. And there is not necessarily a critical mass of fully professional teachers there or, as we've said in the past, teachers and Head Teachers do not always behave in a very professional way. If they have more than one job they don't turn up, they abuse the children, sometimes they're drunk, whatever. That is not a small problem; it's actually quite a widespread problem." (Ed4)

Problems of professionalism are also tied up with the historical legacy of apartheid where schools (teacher and pupils) were part of the anti-apartheid insurgence. There was some praise, however, for the newly introduced Integrated Quality Management System (IQMS).

> "… It is a good start … I think is getting on very well and … we are enthusiastic about it." (HT4)

To sum up then, it might be argued that these *Voices* from South Africa suggest that the education system there 'looks great on paper', but has some complex problems with resources and implementation. Such a summary, however, hides the optimism and pride of many of the interviewees.

KEY POINTS

- There is a strong admiration for government policy (in the form of the 1994 Constitution and in more recent central government legislation). This is matched by an equally strong dissatisfaction about the implementation of policy.

- Educational equity has, thus far, proved to be so disappointingly elusive because of inter-connected: history matters, resources matter and implementation matters.

- In the UK, the GTC (for England, 2005) survey found that when teachers were asked about their sources of frustration, the most commonly cited issue was a perceived sense of *"working in an environment characterised by change which is happening at a fast pace"*.

- *"Education provision is being thought of in systematic terms throughout the world, and there is no doubt that teachers must get used to coming to terms with the external requirements which are bound to ebb and flow over the period of a career".* Pollard (2002:22)

- *Teaching as a Subversive Activity* has even more relevance in today's prescriptive environment.

SIGNPOST

- Schoeman, S. (2006) A blue print for democratic education in South Africa public schools: African teachers' perceptions of good citizenship. *South African Journal of Education*, 26 (1), pp129-142.

POINTS FOR DISCUSSION

- **Pointing the finger** – To what extent is your professional role constrained/supported by Fiske and Ladd's (2004) three issues - the impact of history, resources and implementation?

- **Accepting professional responsibility** - When pointing, three fingers point back to you. Postman and Weingartner (1969) suggest that a vital starting point for new teachers is to consider why you want to be a teacher. Consider both the 'honest' *"I have summers off … I can control people … The pay is good considering the amount of work I do"* and the more challenging answers which reflect your own values – such as, *"as a teacher one can participate in making (sic) intelligence and thereby, in the development of a decent society"*.

- **Reflective Teaching as creative mediation** – Pollard (2002) suggests that *"Reflective Teaching enables teachers to creatively mediate externally developed frameworks for teaching and learning"* (such as the National Curriculum or the National Literacy Strategy). What element(s) of your job need(s) some creative mediation? How can you bring this about? Can you justify your actions … or, your inaction?

CONCLUSION

Whilst, in the UK, the differences between policy and practice are greeted with some cynicism, the South African interviewees' tone was one of disillusion, of disenchantment at the gaps between widely quoted and admired policies and the blatantly obvious flaws in their implementation. The focus of this chapter now turns to examine what student teachers might best be taught about how to respond with professional autonomy to both the problems and the delights which will come their way throughout their career. It was suggested in the introduction that teachers might adopt a Kiplingesque approach by treating both impostors just the same – by meeting both triumphs and disasters with neither cynicism nor optimism, but with a reflective professional autonomy which will allow them to mediate, and, if necessary, subvert whatever may come their way.

All of the South African Educators had a clear fascination with aspects of the ongoing development of the education system in South Africa and some of the head teachers also admired elements of policy. It was refreshing to hear widespread approval for the constitutional arrangements for education. Educators from the UK are more accustomed to a diet of doubt and disparagement about government policy which has in recent years centred around the out-workings of Tony Blair's *'Education, Education, Education'* slogan. Undoubtedly the South African educator who characterised education in the UK as being in a state of inertia is somewhat misguided. On the contrary, there have been a plethora of policy initiatives, many of which have caused despair among teachers and provided endless fodder for the satire of the educational commentator and academic Ted Wragg (2004:1-2):

> *"They (the current Labour Government) came up with a number of good ideas, but then spoiled the effect with some lyrical lunacy … I once upbraided a minister for the rubbish that arrived on Head Teachers' desks every week. 'That's only what gets out', he replied, You should see the stuff I stop".*

Nonetheless, the GTC (2005:10) survey mentioned earlier found that when teachers were asked about their sources of frustration the most commonly cited issue was a perceived sense of *working in an environment characterised by change which is happening at a fast pace.* One head teacher is cited as admiring the initiatives as worthwhile but feeling totally *overwhelmed* by them. In all areas of the UK, the 1990s were characterised, more than any other decade of the twentieth century, by increasingly centralised control of education. In England, this included, for example, the introduction of the *National Literacy Strategy* which *inter alia*, prescribed 15 minutes of text work at whole class level which was to be followed by 15 minutes of word/sentence level work, then 20 minutes of group work, including independent group activities and guided reading and writing, and finally a ten minute plenary to consolidate learning. Whilst such high levels of prescription are rare, Pollard (2002:22) states that *"education provision is being thought of in systematic terms throughout the world, and there is no doubt that teachers must get used to coming to terms with the external requirements which are bound to ebb and flow over the period of a career".*

So how should teachers deal with such ebbs and flows? When moving office recently I discovered three (!) copies of Postman and Weingartner's (1969) seminal work, *Teaching as a Subversive Activity* - clearly this was, at one time, an important text for my predecessor and on reading the chapter about *New Teachers* it is easy to see why. Their 'crap detector' (for questioning content and methods) has even more relevance in today's prescriptive environment. Their suggestions for challenging the mindsets of new teachers are still a recipe for opening minds and ensuring that teachers use their professional autonomy to contribute, not to unquestioning ossification, but to an ever-renewing and vibrant education system.

Pollard (2002) proposes that student teachers should be taught about a particular form of reflective activity which he calls reflective mediation. This involves the interpretation of external requirements in the light of a teacher's understanding of a particular context and bearing in mind his or her values and educational principles.

In a study of change in primary education in the 1990s Osborn *et al* (2000:78) suggest four mediation strategies:

- *Proactive mediation* calls for strategies to defend existing practices that are greatly valued.
- *Innovative mediation* is concerned with teachers finding strategies to work *within* the spaces and boundaries provided by new requirements – finding opportunities to be creative.
- *Collaborative mediation* refers to teachers working closely together to provide mutual support in adapting to and satisfying new requirements. They suggest that the National Curriculum has brought about unprecedented levels of collaboration amongst primary teachers.
- *Conspiratorial mediation* involves schools in adopting more subversive strategies where teachers resist implementing those aspects of external requirements that they believe to be particularly inappropriate.

These forms of mediation come with the health warning that such exercises of professional judgment must be carefully justified. Nonetheless, once armed with a bullet-proof 'crap detector', student teachers should enter the profession prepared, in the face of historical legacy and the limitations of resource and policy implementation, to be both pragmatic and visionary.

REFERENCES

Fiske, E. and Ladd, H. (2004) *Elusive Equity: Education Reform in Post-Apartheid South Africa*. Washington DC: Brookings Institution Press.

Freire, P. (1998) *Teachers as cultural workers: letters to those who dare teach*. Bolder Colorado: Westview Press.

NFER (2005) *General Teaching Council Survey of Teachers 2005*. Slough: NFER.

Osborn, M., McNess, E. and Broadfoot, P. with Pollard, A. and Triggs, P. (2000) *What Teachers Do: Changing Policy and Practice in Primary Education*. London: Continuum.

Pollard, A. (2002) *Reflective Teaching Effective and Evidence Based Professional Practice*. London: Continuum.

Postman, N. and Weingartner, C. (1969) *Teaching as a Subversive Activity*. London: Penguin.

Wragg, T. (2004) *Education, Education, Education: the best bits of Ted Wragg*. London: RoutledgeFalmer.

CHAPTER 3:
WHAT MAKES MEN...?
MASCULINITY, VIOLENCE AND IDENTITY

RICHARD J WOOLLEY,
BISHOP GROSSETESTE UNIVERSITY COLLEGE LINCOLN

"Our leading footballer dresses in skirts, our ... pop idol declares himself gay, and chat shows happily discuss any sexual practice or preference, however recherché. But in spite of the apparent gender liquidity, men seem more preoccupied than ever with the assertion of a male potency." (Coward, 2002)

INTRODUCTION

There is a crisis in masculinity.

In the UK, media portrayals of men appear to show that diversity across a spectrum of masculinities is valued. However, when a political figure admits to being gay this media openness is revealed as being superficial. When a pop star is accused of being gay, he feels it necessary to take legal action in order to clear his name. In the media diverse masculinities (and male sexualities) are not so much welcomed or embraced as tolerated and found conveniently interesting. Publicity about one's sexuality (and thereby, for some, one's perceived masculinity) can still be an unwelcome intrusion and a threat to one's career.

Society has not become as open as it sometimes wishes to appear. It still remains important to boast about sexual activity in order to posture within hegemonic (heterosexual) masculinity and apparent difference is only accepted against the background of a certain sense of what it means to be a man. Connell defines the leading pattern of masculinity as being hegemonic; in other words that which is 'culturally exalted' or 'idealised' (1990:83). This male potency derives from traditional stereotypes of the heterosexual man. Despite moves towards greater equality for all men under Blair's *New Labour* government, including the equalisation of the age of consent and the introduction of civil partnerships, there are still dominant expectations for what constitutes maleness within society.

This chapter will explore some notions of what it means to be male in the settings of South Africa and England. It is exclusive in the sense that it addresses masculinity, although its conclusions will relate to issues of personal identity that may be relevant to all. The focus on men arises from the apparent crisis in male identity, and the significant impact of violence perpetrated by men. The aim is to stimulate discussion about issues that often remain unaddressed in initial teacher education.

TRADITIONS AND STEREOTYPES

Francis identifies that boys are expected to show displays of 'hardness' (2000:100), 'having a laugh' (1999:65), sporting achievement (2000:102), an interest in pastimes and subjects construed as masculine, showing off (2000:107) and non-studious behaviours (Skelton and Francis, 2003:5-7). Whilst this may be the position on the playground, at times the media appears to embrace diverse sexualities. This is reflected in the assertion that masculinities are formed locally and situationally (Connell, cited in Epstein, 2003:9).

Masculinities work at different levels: the national and international level of identifying with heroes and role models, and the local level of finding acceptance and one's place in friendships and community relationships. It is the culture of a society which exerts most influence in the creation of masculine behaviours:

> "You don't have to be the mother of a son to worry about what kind of men we are asking boys to grow into when so many of the old role models are redundant. Male identity has always been built on the subordination of women. If girls are achieving so much more academically, how will boys accommodate women's equality?" (Bunting, 2000)

The increasing success of girls in the English school system, reflected in the now annual debate and comparison between genders when SATs, GCSE and GCE results are published, has brought into question how it is possible to engage boys and to encourage them to see learning as being important. Belying this view is the sense that men have traditionally identified themselves in terms of dominance and superiority, but now find themselves achieving at lower rates than their female counterparts. Traditionally male identity has been derived from a sense of power and from power-relationships:

> "It is important to recognise ... that violence by males against males, which is often interpreted as boys being boys or as bullying, is indeed gender-based. Such violence is often a form of boundary policing, usually with a homophobic edge, which serves to both normalize particular constructions of masculinity while also determining where a boy is positioned within a hierarchical arrangement of masculinities." (Mills, 2001a:4)

In a setting where boys and men are finding themselves achieving less than their female peers, it is important to explore how men develop a sense of maleness and a sense of personal identity in a setting where the tradition of dominance is undermined and untenable:

> "The real boy crisis is a crisis of violence, about the cultural prescriptions that equate masculinity with the capacity for violence." (Foster, Kimmel and Skelton, 2001:16)

Indeed, Skelton (2002:93) suggests that what is required is a move away from stereotypical understandings of what constitutes masculine and feminine, in order to transcend the limitations of sex role theory and appreciate that the gender identities commonly enshrined in male and female bodies are restrictive and now discredited.

When talking about men it is important to remember that they differ a great deal in 'race', location, age, socialisation, family structure and cosmology (Morrell, 2005). Being a man is a diverse, individual and unique experience.

What makes men ... take risks?

Visiting primary schools in the Richmond area of KwaZulu Natal I was surprised by the prominence of materials relating to HIV/AIDS. In my years as a primary school teacher I have been involved in addressing challenging issues with children: alcohol and drug misuse, prejudice, stereotypes and bullying. However, I have never discussed the impact of sexually transmitted diseases, or how such infections are transmitted.

In one classroom a whole display was dedicated to HIV/AIDS. Posters declared *"Use a Condom"*, *"AIDS Kills"* and a list of key messages had been collected by the children on how to tackle child abuse. For these children, aged between 9 and 11 years, HIV/AIDS was not only an issue to be faced in their community, its implications were a daily part of their classroom environment. It was difficult to judge the possible impact of this constant presence on their lives.

A conference held in Durban in 2003 heard of the abuse of female students in schools (Daily News, 2003:1). On average, schools in KwaZulu Natal have an incidence of three student pregnancies each year. Girls were often expected to provide 'sexual favours' in return for responsibilities such as captaining a sports team. In 1998 37% of young people who named their rapist identified a teacher or school Principal; this highlights the importance of tackling such issues directly within the classroom setting. For a female to refuse to have sex is to call into question the male's masculinity. And when this happens, violence frequently results (Morrell, 2001:155). The perpetrators were often teachers, with parents reluctant to press charges and on occasion even taking payment in order to maintain silence:

> *"At boys' camps held as part of a gender, masculinity and HIV and AIDS initiative ... almost all of the 14 to 17 year-olds who attended "defined themselves through their sexual organs."*
> (Daily News, 2003:1)

Male identity is linked implicitly to sexual activity and, in turn, promotes the spread of HIV infection. The high incidence of HIV/AIDS in South Africa has an impact upon identity and the sense of the value of one's humanity. The constant presence of illness and death heightens the sense of the transience of life, and the value that one puts on one's own life. According to the Joint United Nations Programme on HIV/AIDS (UNAIDS), HIV prevalence among South Africans aged 15 to 49 was 21.5% in 2003. This means that 4.3 to 5.9 million people are now living with HIV - the largest number in any country. South Africa also has the world's highest number of rapes: 52,107 cases were reported in 2002, according to police statistics (Sayagues, 2004). It is estimated that around 600 people a day currently die of AIDS-related infections (Ruxton, 2004:217) and eleven teachers die of AIDS-related illnesses each day (MacGregor, 2005:20).

The awareness of one's own sexuality and sexual potency is complicated by the knowledge that the sexual act itself is the primary process of transmitting HIV in South Africa. Issues of HIV/AIDS are discussed in detail in Sue Bermingham's chapter in this volume; the issue here is to consider what the constant presence of death does to young people: death from violence, death from HIV/AIDS, concern about one's own death and the death of one's friends and family:

> *"Questions of masculinity, violence, gender inequity and male sexual power are key to understanding the HIV epidemic in South Africa and to developing responses to it."*
> (Epstein, 2003:3)

In rural settings Iole Matthews (2005) anticipates that increasing poverty, HIV/AIDS and nutritional deficiencies will decimate local communities. Thus the impact of HIV on self-identity, and in this chapter a sense of maleness, cannot be underestimated:

> "This skewed socialisation and lack of self-esteem contribute to increased high-risk sexual encounters. If you are worth nothing in your own eyes, why should you care about your future or that of others? In this context, risking HIV infection and death is a gamble that is easily explicable." (de Keijzer, 2004:105)

It is perhaps no surprise that it is boys and men from working-class and marginalised racial/ethnic backgrounds that are most likely to be hurt. For many boys and men, these forms of masculinity are among the few ways in which they can exert some form of power within a world in which they have very little influence (Mills, 2001b). Applying this notion to the context of South Africa suggests that the risks associated with sexual activity and violence may be outweighed by the need to appear successful, sexually active and powerful:

> "The construction of male identity is still heavily influenced by the legacy of apartheid, for example through the separation and disintegration of families as a result of labour migration. However, it appears also to be closely linked to the spread of the HIV/AIDS epidemic, fuelled by and linked with other factors, such as poverty, violence, and lack of education." (Ruxton, 2004:217)

Furthermore, Morrell (2003) argues that:

> "These steps can be understood as steps of desperation, reflecting their inability to see any other way of dealing with their predicament. Many of these men still believe that they should be good men, responsible fathers and respectful citizens but they cannot see how they can fulfil their social roles in a context where they have nothing and the understanding of a man is that he should provide and protect. Living desperate lives is unlikely to make anybody take safe-sex messages seriously."

The fact that residents of KwaZulu Natal experience 40% unemployment – and in northern areas this can be up to 60-70% (Morrell, 2005) reflects the desperation and frustration faced. KwaZulu Natal has been one of the most violent areas in South Africa, with 50,000 people killed in the five years after the election of Nelson Mandela. Morrell argues that both education in non-violent behaviour and sex education needs to start from the Reception year in school. The history of inequality and struggle in South Africa means that men need to be encouraged to develop a sense of personal identity and to learn how to develop respectful and non-violent relationships with those around them. The violent history of South Africa makes this process complex and difficult for "It is historical experience that defines one's masculinity" (Morrell, 2005). Indeed:

> "One of the greatest challenges is to show boys and girls that they can be friends and not just sexualized others." (Morrell, 2005)

The issues are complex, and further complicated by the legacy of a violent history. Morrell (2003) identifies this as an area for further research and reflection:

> "We need to know a lot more about how heterosexual men who daily confront poverty, understand themselves, how they try and realize their masculinity and how they develop supportive and caring relationships with those around them."

One means of addressing this is for **teacher educators to explore issues with their students in order for them, in turn, to consider self-identity with those in their classrooms.**

WHAT MAKES MEN ... CONFORM?

The risk of being seen as different exerts a great pressure on men to conform to social norms and expectations:

> "Homophobia works to ensure that both heterosexual and homosexual boys who do not conform to the requirements of hegemonic masculinity always have the potential to be subordinated within the social organization of masculinity. The fear of this happening leads many boys to become complicit in maintaining existing gendered power relations."
> (Mills, 2001a:142)

Schools, and particularly individual teachers, have not been prepared or equipped to face issues of sexuality in the classroom. Recent research into the experience of trainee teachers in both South Africa and the UK by Harber and Serf identifies a lack of discussion on key issues relating to sexuality and sexual diversity in both South Africa and the UK:

> "They [the South African students] did not seem to have discussed gender issues, including those of masculinity, at all." (Harber and Serf, unpublished:14)

The English students unanimously said that their courses had done nothing to prepare them to teach about sexuality, for example in relation to HIV/AIDS and homosexuality/homophobia:

> "I don't think the course has prepared anybody for homophobic comments."

> "One student described the area as a 'can of worms', another said that he didn't want to [discuss issues with pupils] because of the potential embarrassment and another that she wouldn't know how to cope with the intimate questions that would be asked."
> (Harber and Serf, unpublished:14)

Unlike students from England, the South African students felt that their courses had informed them about AIDS. However, none of the students, from either country, said they had discussed homosexuality and homophobia.

Harber and Serf argue that student experience does not reflect the claims made by teacher educators in relation to the prominence and delivery of education for democratic citizenship:

> "Few issues are as controversial as race, gender and sexuality but, with the exception of AIDS education in South Africa, insufficient attention is being paid to these areas. On masculinity, homosexuality and homophobia – hardly trivial concerns in a democratic and pluralist society – teacher education in both countries seems to be silent." (unpublished:15)

These teachers in training will encounter homophobic bullying, including name calling, in their classrooms and schools. Although the standards for Qualified Teacher Status (QTS) stipulate that trainees should be able to create safe and secure environments in which learning can flourish, they are not being prepared to tackle issues of identity and diversity. Furthermore:

> "The silences that many schools try to enforce around this topic [homophobia] are a major barrier to counteracting hegemonic masculinizing processes. Homophobia is a very real presence in boys' lives." (Mills, 2001a:142)

Men who have a different view of masculinity from the perceived norm are pressurised into conforming, or at least appearing to conform, to the expectations of those around them.

> "Perhaps the most important consideration when thinking about gender is not biology or psychology or spirituality, but how the idea of gender is used as a tool of social control."
> (Baird, 2004:131)

For male teachers this can lead to a culture of secrecy about their private lives:

> *"Gender-based violence lies at the heart of gender inequality (and racist and homophobic violence), and is rooted in the beliefs of many men about masculinity, and their anxieties about their place in the gender hierarchy."* (Breines *et al*, 2000; Hearn, 1998)

Violence and abuse perpetrated by men is thus a mechanism in asserting power over others and in seeking to ensure that others conform to stereotypical norms. The need to posture within the hierarchy of power relationships leads men to seek dominant positions over others. These issues apply both to the UK and South Africa, although the expression of violence in terms of physical and verbal attacks may vary in each context.

WHAT MAKES MEN ... VIOLENT?

Human Rights Watch (2001) found that sexual violence is experienced by a large proportion of school girls in South Africa, and some estimates suggest that as many as one third of female students have been sexually assaulted in school either by other students or by teachers.

It is a requirement of the South African education system that a student must pass one grade before progressing to the next. Epstein (2003:10) cites the example of a twenty one year old student still in the eleventh grade who also works as a packer at the local supermarket in the evenings and at the weekends, is married and the main breadwinner in the family. Given the fact that female students are more likely to drop out of school due to financial pressures or the need to care for parents and siblings, this exacerbates the problem, increasing the proportion of males within the classroom in high schools. In addition, the presence of older males in the classroom seeking to complete their education affects the balance of power and the breadth of life experience and responsibility encountered by the students. It must also be noted that many other students may have had jobs, some from the age of ten years. Epstein suggests that *"young girls are placed at risk in schools by men in their twenties who are fellow-learners"* (2003:10).

What does this situation say about developing identity, and in this case the development of a sense of masculinity? There is a tension between roles: learner; adult (in a classroom of adolescents); provider; spouse. There are also issues of how one is perceived by oneself and by colleagues in a setting where the majority of peers are younger by six years or more.

The crisis in masculine identity in South Africa arises from a violent hegemony. The origin of this may be traced *"to factors that defined the era of apartheid: marginalisation, poverty, violence, and the forced migration that uprooted men from families and communities"* (Sayagues: 2004). The political and economic inequality that lasted for over forty years contributed to the development of a culture of violence (Harber, 2003:143). *"These social ills transformed male identify into something typified by aggressiveness, risk-taking, sexual prowess and dominance over women"* (Sayagues: 2004).

These notions of masculinity have become entrenched and have continued as post-apartheid men have attempted to find a new place in society, engaging competitively in the quest to take new opportunities and facing frustration as apparent new freedoms have failed to challenge the status quo:

> *"In particular, unemployed men have seen their masculine identities undermined by their lack of work (or work prospects); as a result many have turned to drink, have become increasingly promiscuous, and have abandoned their families."* (Ruxton, 2004:217)

A survey of 30 schools in KwaZulu Natal found that across all 'races' male students and teachers felt uncertain about their role and status. *"For white males, this stemmed in part from the advancement of blacks and women. Black males felt marginalised by poverty, unemployment and women's empowerment."* (Sayagues: 2004)

In schools, a contrast is identified between the approaches of teachers, with the men being portrayed as being unbending, unfeeling, violent, egocentric, competitive, unsympathetic, and rigid. *"These went with the perception that female teachers were prepared to abandon their formal positions of authority to create a climate of understanding and negotiation. Male teachers, on the other hand, were seen as being dogmatically wedded to their authority"* (Morrell, 2001:150). This highlights **the need for teacher educators to address issues of masculinity and power with trainees**.

WHAT MAKES MEN ... BULLY?

Masculinity in both the UK and South Africa is typified by a culture of bullying in schools. In South Africa this appears through physical violence by men towards other men and towards women and children. In the UK it is more apparent in the bullying of males who are perceived as being 'weaker' or 'different' (Rivers, 2000; 2001). When asked, teachers are commonly aware of homophobic incidents in secondary schools. In a survey responded to by 307 teachers in secondary schools in England and Wales, 97% reported being aware of instances of general verbal or physical bullying, 82% were aware of verbal homophobic incidents, and 26% were aware of physical homophobic incidents (Douglas *et al,* 1997). Research in primary schools has been less extensive.

> *"For anti-violence work to have any great success, processes that acknowledge the presence of homophobia in schools and identify it as an unacceptable form of harassment have to be set in motion. This will require significant changes in the ways in which schools have tended to deal with homophobia."* (Mills, 2001a:143)

The National Curriculum for England provides a framework in which it is possible to address issues of inequality, difference, respect and diversity:

> *"Education should have a progressive agenda which would equip children to critique the society they live in and become familiar with contemporary discourses and explanations about inequality so they can develop a range of ideas about solutions."* (Claire, 2001:106)

There are alternative readings of the aims and purposes of citizenship within the National Curriculum. First, citizenship education seeks to educate about public duty, community service and the rules of law and order. Secondly it can seek to evaluate the values, aims and purposes of such activities, to consider equality and justice on a local, societal and global scale:

> *"Thus it is about empowerment, in which children learn to take responsibility for their own lives, and learn how they can influence and participate, not just through conforming but also through their vision of a better world."* (Claire, 2001:106)

This requires schools to develop safe and secure environments in which all children can explore their identities within an understanding that identity is fluid and will develop over time. That only six per cent of schools in England directly address homophobic bullying within their anti-bullying policy is one indication of the sea-change that is required in school cultures (Teachers' TV, 2005).

WHAT MAKES ... MEN'S VALUES?

The constitution of South Africa was adopted on 8th May 1996 (and modified on 11th November 1996). Its preamble states that it seeks to:

- Heal the divisions of the past and establish a society based on democratic values, social justice and fundamental human rights;

- Lay the foundations for a democratic and open society in which government is based on the will of the people and every citizen is equally protected by law;

- Improve the quality of life of all citizens and free the potential of each person; and

- Build a united and democratic South Africa able to take its rightful place as a sovereign state in the family of nations.

The stress on human rights, the equal protection of all people and on releasing the potential of every citizen is ambitious.

Meeting with teachers in Durban it was apparent how aware each person was of the constitution and the ways in which schools were seeking to educate in the light of the ambitious project that South Africa has set for itself. It was surprising how frequently reference was made to the constitution in general conversation, and how teachers were aware of how moves to develop the education system were rooted in that constitution. The optimism that I found amongst primary and secondary school teachers was impressive; there was a real belief in the power of education to transform attitudes and build a new society.

The 1996 Constitution and Bill of Rights guaranteed freedom from discrimination on the grounds of sexual orientation and placed South Africa at the forefront of promoting equality for all people. Carter, Harber and Serf note one outcome of this legislation, from the Lesbian and Gay Equality Project of 2001:

> "The Pretoria High Court has ruled that lesbian and gay couples can now co-adopt children and the Minister for Finance is facing a law suit for his refusal to pay state pensions to the surviving same sex partners of state employees." (2003:35)

South Africa's constitution brought equal rights for all people almost a decade before the introduction, late in 2005, of civil partnerships and equal adoption rights for lesbian and gay couples in England.

The UK does not have a written constitution. However, in the context of education there is a statement of aims, underpinned by values, as the National Curriculum (DfES, 1999:15) seeks to:

(a) provide opportunities for all pupils to learn and to achieve, and

(b) promote pupils' spiritual, moral, social and cultural development and prepare all pupils for the opportunities, responsibilities and experiences of life.

Inherent in these aims are the development of a sense of self-identity and self-worth, creating a safe, secure and stimulating environment in which all can learn, and addressing the whole person: *"the academic study of school subjects cannot be divorced from the formation of pupils as people with feelings, ideas, intuitions, emotions, opinions and beliefs"* (Jacques and Hyland, 2003:126).

The aims of the school system in South Africa contain many similar notions:

> "The Preamble to the South African Schools Act (1996) states that the education system should "redress past injustices in educational provision … contribute to the eradication of poverty … and advance the democratic transformation of society, combat racism and sexism and all other forms of unfair discrimination and intolerance, [and] protect and advance our diverse cultures and languages."
> (West Midlands Commission on Global Citizenship, 2002:26)

However, the National Curriculum for England has a focus on preparing children and young people for future life, and by implication the taking on of a useful and purposeful role within society and the workplace. In contrast, the South African model focuses on the need to eradicate discrimination in all its forms and to protect diversity. At first reading the contrasts may appear subtle. Ending discrimination and valuing all people is implicit to the English model. However, this is dependent on interpretation by the reader. The South African model is far more overt.

The development of these curricula and the motivation and values behind each are discussed elsewhere in this volume by Karen Teasdale. However, what is apparent is that the aspirations of the South African system far outstrip those of the National Curriculum for England. Conversations with teachers confirmed this view; the teachers that I met in South Africa had a far more clearly developed sense of the purposes of education in terms of transforming society than I believe is the case in the UK.

It is important for teacher educators in the UK to help trainees to consider the reasons why they educate. Taking inspiration from the aims of the system in South Africa one may conclude that education is a means through which to diminish (and even eradicate) discrimination. By building self-confidence, nurturing individual potential and fostering a positive self-image it is possible to give children and young people the confidence in who they are so that they can accept the 'different others' they encounter in everyday life. Intolerance is fuelled by ignorance and insecurity.

The bravado of macho and laddish behaviours (Mac an Ghaill, 1994) is one means used by male pupils to protect themselves from those who seek to question or undermine their masculinity. Whatever their stage in developing an understanding of their own sexuality or sexual identity, the pressure to appear to conform to the 'norm' is reflected in the idea that:

> "Becoming somebody is the primary motivation of boys' and girls' social behaviour at school … many boys learn that they must establish their position in a hierarchy of masculinities to avoid being positioned as the marginalized." (Meyenn & Parker, 2001:173)

Various typologies have been suggested to analyse male behaviours in school. Connell (1989) identified the 'cool guys', 'swots' and 'wimps'; Mac an Ghaill (1994) the 'macho lads', the 'academic achievers', the 'new enterprisers' and the 'real Englishmen'; and Martino (1999), using the pupils' own descriptive language to organize findings, the 'cool boys', 'party animals', 'squids' and 'poofters'. Whatever the value of seeking to categorise masculinities, it is clear that there is a continuum. Such diversity is not fixed, and individuals may experience different aspects of being male depending on the setting in which they are operating. It is essential for educators to be aware of this diversity and to consider how they will address such variety in their quest to help each individual find ways of expressing themselves in their own community.

KEY POINTS

- Individuals experience violence on a variety of levels within the education system.

- There are key values and aims underpinning all that schools should seek to achieve; these are open to interpretation.

- Stereotyped masculinity is a means of social control.

- Individuals need to learn and work in safe, secure and supportive environments in which they can explore their own identity and how they relate to the identities of others.

- Teacher-educators need to address complex and controversial issues with their students, and to help build student confidence so that these issues can be explored in schools.

- Men need to explore their dominant, violent and unjust history, and to work to overcome traditional expectations and abuses.

SIGNPOSTS

- Claire, H. (2001) *Not Aliens: Primary School Children and the Citizenship/PSHE Curriculum.* Stoke on Trent: Trentham Books.

- Epstein, D. and Johnson, R. (1998) *Schooling Sexualities.* Buckingham: O.U. Press.

- Epstein, E., O'Flynn, S., and Telford, D. (2003) *Silenced Sexualities in Schools and Universities.* Stoke on Trent: Trentham Books.

- Martino, W. and Meyenn, B. (eds) (2001) *What About the Boys? Issues of Masculinity in Schools.* Buckingham: Open University Press.

- http://www.schools-out.org.uk/ Organisation working for equality for lesbian, gay, bisexual and trans people; resources, news, policy, legal information and networking opportunities.

- http://www.teachers.tv/strandProgramme.do?strandId=6&transmissionProgrammeId =212387 School Matters: Challenging Homophobia. Teachers and students at Turton High School Media Arts College in Bolton and staff and students at Bishop Grosseteste College, Lincoln, discuss how to tackle homophobia and homophobic bullying. First broadcast November 2005.

POINTS FOR DISCUSSION

- How are teachers equipped to help individuals develop a sense of self-identity?

- How do processes, procedures, attitudes and the school curriculum challenge or reinforce traditional stereotypes of masculinity?

- Where do men find role models? How diverse are the positive male role models?

- How can men avoid continuing traditional violent and abusive models of masculinity?

Conclusion

The difficulty with the use of the term masculinity is reflected in the phenomenologists' understanding of the social construction of reality. The term masculine is open to such wide interpretation and varied definition across cultures that it makes any sense of educating for masculinity, or for an awareness of the meaning of masculinity, complex. For the teacher educator the focus should not be on identifying the social norms of masculinity and imparting these, nor should it be on seeking to define (or redefine) the term and to help men and women understand how to promote positive images of masculinity with their students. Rather, the teacher educator should engage with helping teachers and trainee teachers to come to a better understanding of a sense of self, and from this to accept and appreciate the individual attributes of those around them. This understanding must be accompanied by an understanding of society in which diverse and myriad selves contribute to the benefit or detriment of the whole. It is not the isolation of individuals characterised by the neo-conservatism which dominated western society in the late twentieth century; rather it is an appreciation that the whole (society) is more than a sum of all its parts (the individual selves of individual members).

Masculinity is one label that may be used to help individuals consider how they see themselves. However, the power abuses traditionally linked to the term make its usefulness problematic. From the earliest years of schooling, masculinity, and the undermining of an individual's perceived masculinity, is a powerful socialising tool. The taunts of the playground bully make clear what is socially acceptable in terms of being a man, and from this point onwards many males seek to define themselves in terms of the dominant hegemony. Whilst in many societies identity is affected significantly by a sense of being male or female, defining what it means to be masculine (and how others may acceptably express their masculinity) remains one of the major taboos. Whilst it may be possible for one of the nation's greatest footballers to wear his wife's underwear or to appear in public wearing a skirt this is only on the margins of acceptable male behaviour because of the sporting prowess, and thus manliness, that precedes such actions. It is acceptable to be different – but only when you have been accepted or proved yourself. One can easily conjecture that another footballer found behaving in such a manner would find it difficult to gain acceptance in many teams, let alone progress to captain the national squad.

Key questions seek to identify who men are: are you married; do you have children; are you a virgin? Each one seeks to explore the masculinity of the respondent. Implicit to each is the question *"are you a man?"* with all the traditional senses of what that entails. Such questions can come from many stakeholders in a school. Whilst there is a strong tradition of single female teachers, and indeed at points in history it was required that a female teacher remain unmarried, in contemporary society there is a sense that women may remain single because they have chosen to pursue a career. For the male teacher there is still a stigma associated with being single and of having no clear evidence of heterosexual credentials. Anecdotal evidence suggests to me that even at the stage of training to teach, male students feel a sense of pressure because they are viewed as being unusual for choosing to work with children. This is particularly apparent amongst those training to work in the early years of primary education (Carrington, 2002:301). What does this suggest about the way in which masculinity is perceived by many in society (including parents/carers, children and colleagues) and about the needs of trainees in developing their own self-identity and self-confidence during their programme of study?

Recent studies suggest that boys do not benefit from having male teachers; they benefit from good teaching. Of course, this can include good teaching from male practitioners. However, the stigma associated with becoming a male primary school teacher requires that training providers address the need for students to develop a clear and confident sense of self-identity as a part of developing as reflective, confident and self-assured practitioners. This applies to both England and South Africa, as both settings face a shortage of male primary school teachers.

This issue of identity is important. I am not arguing for the promotion of any kind of gender identity or sexuality. However, I do believe that schools should be welcoming and open places where all stakeholders can explore their identities free from bullying and harassment. The notion of respect for all people, and the understanding that all people are different, are key to this discussion. Whilst the issues are complex and will certainly cause us to face challenging situations, for teachers and teacher educators the challenge is to engage in the debate and to promote the value of diversity. Issues surrounding identity have been neglected, or avoided as taboo; the silence needs to end and the debate to begin.

The sense that schools are violent places (Harber, 2003) makes this all the more important. If traditional masculinity is associated with violence and the abuse of power, then male teachers need to reconceptualise their own identities as men so that they can break the spiral of stereotypical maleness. In addition, all teachers need to be aware of the continuum of sexualities and gender identities in order to create environments in which pupils and staff can develop a sense of self. The complicity of the education system and the media makes this a difficult task.

> "A school's role in the formation of masculinity needs to be understood in two ways, for as well as providing the setting and physical space in which the embodied actions and agencies of pupils and adults take place, its own structures and practices are also involved as an institutional agent that produces these 'masculinizing practices.'" (Swain, 2006:333-4)

Men have to face up to their past. Not only as individuals, but as a homogenous group that has benefited from a dominant position in many societies over many generations. It is like a nation facing up to the abuses of Imperialism. Whilst some men have been abused and marginalised, others, and the majority, have benefited from social systems and traditions that have enabled them to dominate and violate others. This can no longer be the norm. There is a need for repentance, forgiveness, rethinking and discussion. While ever some men continue to see themselves as the dominant force within society, abuses and violence will continue. Men need to see themselves in a different light; to consider how they will allow other men to discover diverse masculinities; and to explore how they can relate to women and children in ways that value the shared humanity of all.

The ambitions and vision found within the South African education system offer challenges and hope to those willing to engage in the process. **South Africa may have started on a long journey, but in the UK the silences and taboos need to be broken too.**

REFERENCES

Baird, V. (2004) *Sex, Love and Homophobia: Lesbian, Gay, Bisexual and Transgender Lives*. London: Amnesty International.

Breines, I., Connell, R., and Eide, I. (2000) *Male Roles, Masculinities and Violence: A Culture of Peace Perspective.* Paris: UNESCO Publishing.

Bunting, M. (2000) *Masculinity in Question* in The Guardian, 02/10/00, 2000 http://www.guardian.co.uk/comment/story/0,,376019,00.html

Carrington, B. (2002) A Quintessentially Feminine Domain? Student Teachers' Constructions of Primary Teaching as a Career. *Educational Studies*, 28,3, pp287-303.

Carter, C., Harber, C., and Serf, J. (2003) *Towards Ubuntu: Critical Teacher Education for Democratic Citizenship in South Africa and England.* Birmingham: Development Education Centre.

Claire, H. (2001) *Not Aliens: Primary School Children and the Citizenship/PSHE Curriculum.* Stoke on Trent: Trentham Books.

Connell, R. W. (1989) "Cool Guys, Swots and Wimps": The Interplay of Masculinity and Education. *Oxford Review of Education*, 15, pp291-303.

Connell, R. W. (1990) An Iron Man: The Body and Some Contradictions of Hegemonic Masculinity in Messner, M and Babo, D. (1990) *Sport, Men and the Gender Order: Critical Feminist Perspectives.* Champaign, Illinois: Human Kinetics Books.

Coward, R. *Boys Must Still be Boys* in The Guardian, 12/0302
http://www.guardian.co.uk/comment/story/0,,665862,00.html

Daily News. November 26, 2003. South Africa.

De Keijzer, B. (2004) Masculinities: Resistance and Change in Ruxton, S. (ed) (2004) *Gender Equality and Men: Learning from Practice.* London: Oxfam GB.

DfES (1999) *National Curriculum for Primary Schools in England.* London: DfES/QCA.

Douglas, N., Warwick, I., Kemp, S., and Whitty, G. (1997) *Playing it Safe: Responses of Secondary School Teachers to Lesbian and Gay Pupils, Bullying, HIV and AIDS Education and Section 28.* London: Terrence Higgins Trust.

Epstein, D. (2003) Gender, Sexuality and Identity: Violence and HIV in South African Schools, *in ESRC Seminar Series*, Warwick 15th February 2003. Unpublished typescript.

Foster, V., Kimmel, M., and Skelton, C. (2001) What About the Boys? An Overview of the Debates in Martino, W. and Meyenn, B. (eds) (2001) *What About the Boys? Issues of Masculinity in Schools.* Buckingham: Open University Press.

Francis, B. (1999) *Boys, Girls and Achievement: Addressing the Classroom Issues.* London: RoutledgeFalmer.

Harber, C. (2001) Schooling and Violence in South Africa: Creating a Safer School. *Intercultural Education*, 12 (3), pp261-271.

Harber, C. (2003) Schools, Democracy and Violence in South Africa in Osler A. (ed) *Citizenship and Democracy in Schools.* Stoke on Trent: Trentham Books.

Harber C. and Serf J. (2006) Teacher Education for a Democratic Society. *Teaching and Teacher Education*, 22 (8), forthcoming.

Hearn, J. (1998) *The Violences of Men: How Men Talk About and How Agencies Respond to Men's Violence to Women.* London: Sage.

Human Rights Watch (2001) *Scared at School: Sexual Violence Against Girls in South African Schools.* New York: Human Rights Watch.

Jacques, K. and Hyland, R. (2003) *Professional Studies: Primary Phase.* Exeter: Learning Matters.

Kehily, M. and Swann, J. (2003) *Children's Cultural Worlds.* Chichester: John Wiley.

Le Grange, G. (2004) Taking the Bull by the Horns: Working with Young Men on HIV/AIDS in South Africa in Ruxton, S. (ed) *Gender Equality and Men: Learning from Practice.* London: Oxfam GB.

Mac an Ghaill, M. (1994) *The Making of Men.* Buckingham: Open University Press.

MacGregor, K. (2005) Alarm Sounds as AIDS Claims 11 Teachers a Day. *Times Education Supplement* 15/04/05.

Martino, W. (1999) "Cool boys," "party animals," "squids" and "poofters": Interrogating the dynamics and politics of adolescent masculinities in school. *British Journal of Sociology of Education,* 20, pp239-63.

Martino, W and Meyenn, B. (eds) (2001) *What About the Boys? Issues of Masculinity in Schools.* Buckingham: Open University Press.

Matthews, I. (2005) (10th August) *Introduction to the Independent Projects Trust*. Durban: Independent Projects Trust.

Meyenn, B. and Parker, J. (2001) Naughty Boys at School: Perspectives on Boys and Discipline *in* Martino, W. & Meyenn, B. (eds) (2001) *What About the Boys? Issues of Masculinity in Schools*. Buckingham: Open University Press.

Mills, M. (2001a) *Challenging Violence in Schools: an issue of masculinities*. Buckingham: Open University Press.

Mills, M. (2001b) Pushing it to the max: interrogating the risky business of being a boy *in* Martino, W. & Meyenn, B. (eds) (2001) *What About the Boys? Issues of Masculinity in Schools*. Buckingham: Open University Press.

Morrell, R. (2001) Corporal Punishment and Masculinity in South African Schools. *Men and Masculinity*, 4 (2), pp140-157.

Morrell, R. (2003) *'Poverty and HIV'*, contribution to UN web discussion on the HIV/AIDS pandemic, 11/0703, http://esaconf.un.org/~gender-equality-role-men-boys/guests

Morrell, R. (2005) (11th August) *Masculinity*. Durban: University of KwaZulu Natal.

Rivers, I. (2000) Social Exclusion, Absenteeism and Sexual Minority Youth. *Support for Learning*, 15 (1), pp13-17.

Rivers, I. (2001) The Bullying of Sexual Minorities at School: Its Nature and Long-term Correlates. *Educational and Child Psychology*, 18 (1), pp33-46.

Ruxton, S. (ed) (2004) *Gender Equality and Men: Learning from Practice*. London: Oxfam GB.

Salie, I. Focus on Boys to Stamp Out Family Violence *Saturday Argus*, p. 14, 20/11/04 http://www.int.iol.co.za/index.php?set_id=1&click_id=13&art_id=vn20041120115904347C462918

Sayagues, M. (2004) Undermining South Africa's Culture of Violence. *Mail & Guardian Online* 20/09/04 http://www.mg.co.za/articlepage.aspx?articleid=137648&area=/insight/insight__national/

Skelton, C. (2002) The 'Feminisation of Schooling' or 'Re-masculinising' Primary Education? *International Studies in Sociology of Education*, 12 (1), pp77-96.

Skelton, C. (2001) *Schooling the Boys: Masculinities and Primary Education*. Buckingham: Open University Press.

Skelton, C. and Francis, B. (eds) (2003) *Boys and Girls in the Primary Classroom*. Maidenhead: Open University Press.

Swain, J. (2006) Reflections on Patterns of Masculinity in School Settings. *Men and Masculinities*, 8 (3), pp331.249.

Teachers' TV (2005) *School Matters: Challenging Homophobia*. http://www.teachers.tv/strandProgramme.do?strandId=6&transmissionProgrammeId=212387 broadcast 24/11/05.

West Midlands Commission on Global Citizenship (2002) *Whose Citizenship? Exploring Identity, Democracy and Participation in a Global Context*. Birmingham: Development Education Centre.

Chapter 4:
HIV/AIDS
The most serious threat to international security

Sue Bermingham, Manchester Metropolitan University

Introduction

This 21st century health issue affecting teachers and pupils is not contained by political borders. In Kenya the figures are similar to South Africa with estimates of 10 teachers dying each week from AIDS, and in Zambia AIDS claims the lives of approximately 2,000 teachers a year, more than the output of the country's teacher training colleges, with about half the newly trained teachers dying each year from AIDS.

New hotspots of HIV/AIDS are emerging in China, India, Russia, Nigeria and Ethiopia. Figures for the UK (more than 7,750 diagnosed in 2005 almost 500 more than in 2004, Telegraph 27/1/06) are showing a recent rise in cases of HIV infection. *"HIV/AIDS is 'the most serious threat to international security known to humankind'."* (Furniss, 2006:47)

The Human Immuno-deficiency Virus (HIV) and Acquired Immuno-Deficiency Syndrome (AIDS) were first named in the early 1980s, since when the numbers infected have soared, with approximately 37.8 million living with HIV in 2001 and over 40 million in 2004. By 2010 there could be over 100 million infected.

All UN countries agreed to the eight Millennium Development Goals. Goal 6 aims to combat HIV/AIDS, malaria and other diseases, with a target to have halted and started to reverse the spread by 2015. In June 2001 all 189 member governments of the UN signed the UN General Assembly Special Session (UNGASS) Declaration of Commitment, promising action on HIV/AIDS *"in the fields of leadership, prevention, care and support, treatment, reducing vulnerability, and human rights'"* and to implement national strategies to support AIDS orphans and children with HIV/AIDS *"by providing appropriate counseling and psychosocial support, ensuring their enrolment in school and access to shelter, good nutrition and health and social services on an equal basis with other children."* http://www.un.org/ga/aids/coverage/

World leaders at the G8 summit in July 2005 agreed to provide a range of support. By the end of that year the US Department of Health and Human Services approved new sources of low cost, high quality ART (anti-retrovirals) drugs from India and South Africa, and in March 2006 the World Health Organisation approved three more sources of anti-retrovirals and two anti-malarials, thus increasing the supply of appropriate medical treatment.

There is at least a glimmer of hope in the battle to contain and reduce the impact of HIV/AIDS; more political support, more funding and more drugs are available. This is 20 years after the World Health Organisation stated that HIV/AIDS is *"a pandemic as mortal as any pandemic there has ever been"* and they pledged their *"energy, commitment and creativity to the urgent, difficult and complex task of global AIDS prevention and control".* (Furniss, 2006:50)

HIV/AIDS in South Africa

South Africa remains top of the dismal statistics concerning HIV/AIDS with the largest number of victims of HIV/AIDS in the world. It is estimated that 6 million South Africans will be HIV positive by 2010 (Worldwatch Institute, 2005). Other African countries appear to have successfully managed the HIV/AIDS crisis and are reporting reduced prevalence rates e.g. Uganda, Senegal and Kenya. Governments need to be sensitive and open in order to tackle HIV/AIDS. The whole issue of HIV/AIDS is surrounded by controversy involving 'taboo' subjects such as sex and drugs, as well as a range of views as to its origin (http://www.avert.org/origins.htm). For many cultures it is alien for a government to advise on sexual practices but the longer a government ignores the issue the more people will become infected.

> "HIV and AIDS was just a monster that you couldn't talk about because of the way it's transmitted, because it involved sex. We couldn't talk about it among ourselves as teachers because of stigma. We couldn't talk about it to the pupils because we were part of the apartheid homeland system and the department of education didn't want us to talk about condoms. They thought it would encourage sex."
>
> Mbetse South African Democratic Teachers Union quoted by McGreal in South African Mail and Guardian 20th December 2005

The socio-economic impacts of HIV/AIDS are immense. The virus affects mainly the working age group, leaving dependants (especially children) vulnerable.

> "AIDS sets off a vicious spiral. As adults die, families grow poorer. As families grow poorer, children grow hungry. When children are hungry, they grow weak and vulnerable to infectious diseases. If they have inherited HIV from their mothers, this leaves them more vulnerable still ... More children will drop out of school to care for dying parents, earn a living, do household chores or raise younger siblings. Missing out on school will make them ignorant about sex, AIDS and condoms." (Guest, 2003:157)

After decades of improving quality of life and life expectancy, some countries have already reported falling life expectancy rates in the 21st century. The main reason is HIV/AIDS. The life expectancy at birth in South Africa has reduced from 62 years (born 1990-1995) to an expected 42 years (born 2005-10). At present (born 2000-2005) the life expectancy without AIDS would be 67 years, with AIDS it is 49 years (UN population division).

Post-1994 South African governments have made attempts to manage HIV/AIDS though not all of the strategies have been successful. In 1996 over R14 million (approx £1.4 million) was spent on a musical to raise awareness of AIDS. Unfortunately, the poorest could not afford the ticket prices. In 1997 the government backed Virodene, a 'miracle' cure that turned out to be an industrial solvent. (Guest, 2003:65)

South Africa has been 'reborn' post apartheid and is making major educational changes. The educational system has had two massive influences on it – the new outcomes-based, education for all policies (http://www.education.gov.za/) with citizenship at its heart, and HIV/AIDS. South Africa has increased its spending on education with 5.5% GDP spent on education in 2002 compared to the UK spending 4.6% of its GDP on education (Nunn, 2005). However,

> "Efforts to build an educational system in a post-apartheid era are being stymied by the loss of personnel to the disease, and a severe shortage of teachers and professors over the next decade is anticipated." (Worldwatch Institute, 2005)

"... you will find classrooms where for half a year there are no teachers and most of the students are sick or are taking care of sick parents." (Zewdie, 2005)

HIV/AIDS is killing teachers and pupils. The ELRC report (2005) estimated that over 12% of South African public school teachers are HIV positive. Botswana has reduced its teacher-training programme from 3 years to 6 months in order to keep enough teachers in the system.

Visiting schools in KwaZulu Natal during August 2005 we could not fail to notice the lists of absent pupils on the blackboards. Many pupils arrive in school stressed from caring for sick parents, under nourished and exhausted from working to keep the family afloat.

The increasing number of orphans is another real issue for South African schools. A survey of 250 schools found 23-24% of enrolled pupils are orphans - single, double or missing parents (Badcock-Walters, 2005). In the poignant book *Children of AIDS: Africa's Orphan Crisis* (Guest, 2003), it is estimated that out of a population of nine million people in KwaZulu Natal province there will be 500,000 orphans by 2010. The HIV/AIDS epidemic needs curbing now, with HIV prevention messages incorporated into projects with street children as well as through formal education. Guest argues that the best place for orphans is within their own communities. This places an immense burden on the poorest communities that are unemployed, impoverished, old and largely female (*ibid*. page 11).

Badcock–Walters (2005) highlight the following trends for South African pupils:

- Enrolment decline (fertility rates down, HIV positive women 30% less likely to fall pregnant)
- Increasing attrition of pupils
- Increased learner/educator ratios
- Female vulnerability – girls as carers, and vulnerable to HIV infection
- Decreased transition rates from primary to secondary education

Within the South African educational system the stigma surrounding HIV/AIDS is similar to the historical treatment of leprosy victims. Within the UK the stigma and fear was more around sexual practices. Fortunately the climate has changed and in both societies there is a more open willingness to care for HIV/AIDS victims. In South Africa the death of Gugu Dlamini by stoning after her courage in admitting her infection, plus high profile cases such as Nelson Mandela's eldest son, has led to changes. In the centre of Durban lies the Gugu Dlamini Park honouring her courage.

VIEWS OF STUDENT TEACHERS IN THE UK

Trainee teachers at Manchester Metropolitan University studying the one year Post Graduate Certificate in Education course (academic year 2005-2006) were asked, 4 months into their course, whether they thought controversial issues were important to them as teachers and to the pupils they are training to teach. Their responses included comments relating to their role.

Educating the next generation for this planet they share and will be part responsible for.

- Controversial topics should be taught as it is these issues that could shape the world of the future.
- Controversial issues such as HIV/AIDS should be studied by all, as many are issues of global responsibility, which all should be responsible for.
- Teaching controversial issues should be integrated into all subjects to prepare pupils for later life and to help them explore complex issues relating to other people.

As educators promoting and valuing equal opportunities amongst their classes.

- Controversial issues permeate the teaching experience. In many instances these issues will arise in the course of a scheme of work for Geography, Citizenship, RE etc. However, they will also arise from the lives and different experiences of pupils in the school. Teachers need to be taught how to carefully and delicately deal with these issues.
- It is important for trainee teachers to be able to use their subject as a tool for unlocking pupils' thoughts on controversial issues.
- Controversial issues should be used across the curriculum. They allow pupils to develop their own values and opinions. They allow them to be independent thinkers.

Within the safe environment of the classroom of tackling real issues.

- Yes, I think that controversial issues should be taught as they are real issues which should be addressed in an open, non-threatening environment e.g. classroom.
- All trainees should be exposed to controversial issues such as AIDS as you can never know when an issue may arise in the classroom and having the knowledge of how to deal with such occurrences is paramount.
- Controversial issues are part of day to day life in communities. Teachers need to be able to enable learners to access different, contrasting and often conflicting value systems.
- Controversial issues should be taught because children encounter them throughout their adolescence through media, from talking about them with their peers. By teaching about them we can help to reduce stereotypes.

"Understandably some teachers, particularly newly qualified teachers, may lack confidence when approaching these issues." (DFEE, 1998:60)

THE ROLE OF TEACHER EDUCATORS AND TEACHERS

In countries such as South Africa, teachers play a crucial role in helping to halt the spread of HIV/AIDS.

> "In October, South Africa's four teachers' trade unions launched a multimillion dollar scheme in thousands of schools, with US government financing, to get AIDS talked about among teachers, by teachers to their pupils - and, above all, to save teachers' lives."
> (McGreal, 2005:2)

Visiting Durban and Richmond classrooms it was noticeable that most had colourful HIV/AIDS posters including:

- *My friend with HIV & AIDS is still my friend* Calendar from the KZN Department of Education Life Skills HIV & AIDS Unit;

- *... Please if you have put yourself at risk for HIV/AIDS do not donate blood* from the South African National Blood Service;

- *AIDS Kills* hand written posters with a local AIDS helpline phone number.

This is good news. Information to help school children take preventative measures is becoming more widely available.

The National Framework for Teacher Education in South Africa (Department of Education, 2005:15) has a recommendation for all ITE courses to prioritise *"a definite focus on HIV and AIDS – including the development of an informed understanding of the pandemic and its impacts on schooling and community life, and the competencies to cope responsibly with the effects of the pandemic in learning sites."*

Teachers in Europe also need to be equipped to deal sensitively with HIV positive pupils. Thorne *et al* (2000) have carried out research relating to the disclosure of HIV infection status in seven European countries including the UK. As anti-retroviral treatment (ART) for HIV positive pregnant women in Europe has improved, less than 10% of children born (to HIV positive mothers) will be HIV positive. This is good news for the 90% born free of infection, yet these children will lose one or both parents to AIDS before or during adolescence. With ARTs the children born infected have a good chance of living into adolescence. The research highlights that only 11% of the HIV positive parents had disclosed their own infection status to their child, and only 18% of the HIV positive children had been told of their status. Only 60% of the HIV positive children aged 11 years or older had been told. The findings support the USA figures in which 50% of HIV positive 11 year olds enrolled in clinical trials had not been told of their status (Brady *et al* 1996). **These figures underline the silences surrounding HIV/AIDS.**

The UK media headlines at the start of 2006 are concerned with fuel supplies, especially gas, and the threat of Bird Flu. HIV/AIDS does not seem to get a mention in the media. Is it such a global issue? Should it concern teacher educators in the UK?

The children in all our classrooms need to know about HIV/AIDS for their own sakes as well as in helping to understand and empathise with others. This is not an easy topic to teach in the classroom as it involves sex, drugs and religion. To ignore it is to put children at risk.

The QCA Citizenship Schemes of Work – Teachers' Booklet (QCA, 2001: Appendix 9) has guidance on the teaching of sensitive and controversial issues. Issues that are likely to be sensitive or controversial are those that have: political, social or personal impact; arouse strong feelings; and deal with questions of value or belief. It includes examples such as: sex education; religion; politics; family lifestyle and values; unemployment; and bereavement.

HIV/AIDS can be used to explore all of the above. The study of controversial issues is not the monopoly of 'Citizenship' education, but an essential element of all curriculum areas. Subjects such as Geography have a role to play in encouraging *"on the part of the individual a readiness to participate in solving problems of their communities, their countries and the world at large."* (Hartwig and Haubrich,1999).

One of the main fears of teachers is that they will be criticised (by parents, governors and others) for the way they handle controversial issues within their classrooms.

GUIDANCE ON TEACHING CONTROVERSIAL ISSUES

The Advisory Group on Citizenship (1998) offers guidance on the teaching of controversial issues:

We acknowledge, however, that in the teaching of controversial issues there is always a risk of bias, whether unwitting or otherwise. Experienced teachers would seek to avoid this by resisting any inclination to:

- highlight a particular selection of facts or items of evidence thereby giving them a greater importance than other equally relevant information;

- present information as if it is not open to alternative interpretation or qualification or contradiction;

- set themselves up as the sole authority not only on matters of 'fact' but also on matters of opinion;

- present opinions and other value judgements as if they are facts;

- give their own accounts of the views of others instead of using the actual claims and assertions as expressed by various interest groups themselves;

- reveal their own preferences by facial expression, gestures or tone of voice;

- imply preferences by a particular choice of respondents or by not opening up opportunities for all pupils to contribute their views to a discussion;

- neglect challenging a consensus of opinion which emerges too readily.

(DFEE, 1998 section 10.9:58)

The DFEE guidance could be used by student teachers when critically analysing a videoed lesson on HIV/AIDS, or with peer observation.

Since 1988 December 1st has been designated World AIDS day, and is promoted in a growing number of countries. In 2005 children from over 50 countries took part in 'Lessons for Life' learning more about HIV/AIDS. http://www.gmfc.org

Recent research by Oulton *et al* (2004) of UK schools in the Midlands, South and London areas found 60% of secondary school teachers and 70% of primary school teachers had had no formal training (ITE or INSET) to teach controversial issues. Only 10% (of the 205 respondents) had pre service training. Do we prepare trainee teachers to deal with controversial, sensitive issues?

Many UK ITE courses have a Professional Studies module in which trainees have lectures and seminars around social and cultural issues that affect all teachers. The one Year PGCE Handbook at Manchester Metropolitan University, for example, says *"You will often be discussing sensitive and possibly controversial issues in professional studies and therefore it is important to remember that everyone has the right to an opinion, the right to be heard and the right to disagree."* The handbook goes on to remind students that alongside freedom of speech everyone needs to abide by the Equal Opportunities Policy as well as common courtesies and professional ethics.

The DFEE (2000:2/3) Guidance booklet *Developing a global dimension in the school curriculum* highlights eight key concepts:

- Citizenship
- Social Justice
- Diversity
- Sustainable Development
- Values and Perceptions
- Interdependence
- Conflict Resolution
- Human Rights

Midwinter's handbook (2005) *Supporting the Standards* highlights opportunities of how the eight key concepts (above) can be developed. Exemplars from a range of ITE providers demonstrate how to embed the global dimension from professional development days (Bath Spa University), to Primary trainees using environmental issues to develop Year 5 Literacy skills (Swansea Institute of Higher Education). This is an invaluable 31 pages full of advice, sharing resources and good practice.

So how does a teacher educator handle controversial issues? Harwood (1986) identified a range of roles:

1. Impartial Facilitator (impartial chairing, asks open questions, neutral response to pupil's ideas);
2. Instructor (states ideas, opinions as matters of fact not for discussion, closed questions);
3. Devil's Advocate (deliberately provocative statements or questions);
4. Task Supervisor (manages the task rather than content/issues).

A possible activity with student teachers could involve group work with the stimulus of a newspaper headline concerning HIV/AIDS, to devise differing viewpoints for pupils to debate, and to carefully consider the role the teacher could take.

The Geographical Association Website www.geography.org.uk contains advice for teacher educators concerning the global dimensions in courses. One link takes you to *Geography: The global dimension (Key Stage 3).* The materials are jointly published by the DEA and the GA and contains a useful *PLANNING TOOL KIT* which can be used to prompt a student teacher when planning a unit of work to carefully consider questions such as:

- Values and attitudes – does the work help learners to explore their own values?
- Skills – does it enable learners to be more effective in bringing about change?
- Knowledge and understanding – does it demonstrate links between global issues and the learners' own experiences?
- Integrity – does it respect the human rights of the pupils and of others?

CONCLUSION

The Synoptic A2 Geography exam paper January 2006 for AQA (UK) focused on HIV/AIDS with statistics and maps highlighting the global picture and providing case study details on Zambia. This is a welcome recognition of the issue, but **teachers must ensure is that children in countries such as the UK do not develop the idea that HIV/AIDS is 'over there' rather than a global issue to be tackled by all.**

GOOD PRACTICE INDICATORS

Education for an interdependent world
ITET courses should explore the challenges and opportunities of educating teachers for a global society.

Development of Political literacy
ITET courses should seek to develop students' understanding of political and decision-making processes at a local, national and international level, e.g. G8 or the UN.

Values and attitudes
ITET courses should encourage students to explore their own and other people's values and attitudes on issues to do with HIV/AIDS.

Subject Knowledge
ITET courses should ensure that students have the knowledge (of HIV/AIDS) and skills to tackle controversial issues.

Research and scholarship
ITET courses should promote action research and other investigations into the theory and practice surrounding HIV/AIDS in teaching and learning.

School Policy
ITET courses should encourage and support students to engage in debate about controversial issues such as HIV/AIDS and educational policy in the schools where they work.

(adapted from Bennell *et al*, 2004:54)

For teachers in South Africa HIV/AIDS affects their practice on a daily basis. They have constant reminders, such as classroom posters and articles in newspapers. Teachers can also be personally touched by the issue, losing colleagues, friends, family and pupils to the disease.

ITE courses in South Africa need to prepare trainee teachers to cope in an education system that is preparing pupils for their place in the global society, at the same time as providing pupils with the knowledge and skills to cope in a society ravaged by HIV/AIDS.

ITE providers in the UK cannot be complacent about HIV/AIDS. This is a global issue that is important here too. ITE courses need to equip trainee teachers with the knowledge and skills to enable pupils to explore the issues and understand the implications.

KEY POINTS

- HIV/AIDS is a global issue affecting teachers and pupils.

- Teachers can play a vital role in making this issue open and discussed.

- Teaching controversial issues is not easy.

- Trainee teachers need to be given the tools, information and strategies to tackle controversial issues in their classrooms.

- Teachers need continuing professional development.

- There is growing support and guidance available to teacher educators.

SIGNPOSTS

- www.geography.org.uk especially the GTIP (Geography Trainers' Induction Programme) section which includes exemplars of ITE sessions.

- www.gmfc.org/ Global Movement for Children is worth a closer look and includes videos on HIV/AIDS and lesson suggestions for Worlds AIDS Day.

- Midwinter, C. (2005) *The Global Dimension in Initial Teacher Education and Training Supporting the Standards,* World Studies Trust – shares ideas and strategies employed by a range of ITE courses.

- Price, J. (2001) *Who decides? Citizenship through Geography,* ActionAid & DFID. Pages 40-70 consider HIV & AIDS in Uganda with teachers' information and lots of classroom activities.

- www.un.org/millenniumgoals/ Details on the eight Millennium Goals, and ongoing progress towards achieving them.

- Harwood, D. L. (1986) To advocate or to educate? What role for the teacher in political education in the primary years? *Education 3–13,* 14 (1), 51–7. Harwood, D. L. (1989) The nature of teacher–pupil interaction in the Active Tutorial Workapproach: Using interaction analysis to evaluate student-centred approaches. *British Educational Research Journal* 15 (2), 177–94. Global Citizenship Guides – Teaching Controversial Issues (2006:7) Oxfam *The Role of the Teacher* describes six roles based on Harwood's work.

POINTS FOR DISCUSSION

- Do your ITE /CPD courses prepare trainees to tackle controversial issues?

- Do your trainees have access to a range of information and teaching and learning strategies for teaching the issue of HIV/AIDS?

- Can a 'balanced' approach be achieved when teaching HIV/AIDS?

REFERENCES

Badcock-Walters, P. (2005) *HIV/AIDS Impact on The Education Sector The Management Challenge* presentation to group on visit to Durban, August 2005.

Bennell, S. *et al* (2004) *The Improving Practice Series: Global Perspectives and Teachers in Training*. London: DEA.

Bowden, R. & Binns, T. (2001) *The Changing Face of South Africa*. London: Hodder Wayland.

Department of Education (2005) *A National Framework for Teacher Education in South Africa, Report of the Ministerial Committee on Teacher Education*. Pretoria: Department of Education, Republic of South Africa.

DfEE (1998) *Education for Citizenship and the teaching of democracy in schools. Final Report of the Advisory Group on Citizenship*. London: DfEE/QCA.

DfEE (2000) *Developing a global dimension in the school curriculum*. London: DfEE/QCA.

DfEE (1999) *The National Curriculum Handbook for secondary teachers in England*. London: DfEE/QCA.

DfES/TTA (2002) *Qualifying to Teach - Professional Standards for Qualified Teacher Status*. London: DfES/TTA.

Education Labour Relations Council (2005) *Factors Determining Educator Supply and Demand in South African Public Schools*. Cape Town, South Africa: Human Science Research Council.

Furniss, C. (2006) AIDS Crisis 25 years on. *Geographical Magazine*, 78 (1).

Guest, E. (2003) *Children of AIDS, Africa's orphan crisis*. London: Pluto Press.

Hartwig and Haubrich (1992) Charter - International Geographical Union (IGU) CGE Charter on Geographical Education & 2006 draft accessed at igu-cge.tamu.edu/cgecharter2005.pdf

MacGregor, K. (15/4/05) *'Alarm sounds as AIDS claims 11 teachers a day'* TES accessed 28th December 2005 www.tes.co.uk/search/story/?story_id=2090757

McGreal, C. (2005) Young teachers are dying, *The Guardian/Education Guardian*, 20/12/2005, p5.

Manchester Metropolitan University (2005) One Year PGCE Handbook

Midwinter, C. (2005) *Supporting the Standards. The Global Dimension in Initial Teacher Education and Training*. Manchester: DFID & The World Studies Trust.

Nunn, A. (April 2005) *The 'Brain Drain' Academic and Skilled Migration to the UK and its Impacts on Africa*. Report to the AUT and NATFHE Policy Research Institute Faculty of Business and Law. Leeds Metropolitan University, 22 Queen Square, Leeds, LS2 8AF www.leedsmet.ac.uk/lbs/pri accessed from www.aut.org.uk/index.cfm?articleid=1351

Oulton, C., Day, V., Dillon, J. and Grace, M. (2004) Controversial issues – teachers' attitudes and practices in the context of citizenship education. *Oxford Review of Education*, 30 (4).

QCA (2001) *Citizenship Schemes of Work – Teachers' Booklet*. London: QCA.

Telegraph 27/1/06 via Info Trac Web: Customs Newspapers CJ141329638

Thorne, C., Newell, M-L. and Peckham, C. S. (2000) Disclosure of diagnosis and planning for the future in HIV-affected families in Europe. *Child Care, Health and Development*, 26 (1) pp29-40.

Young, H. (ed) (2004) *Geography: The global dimension (Key Stage 3)*. DEA: London

Zewdie, D. (2005) *New Plan to Fight HIV/AIDS* World Bank's Global HIV/AIDS Program Director accessed July 8th 2006 at: web.worldbank.org/WBSITE/EXTERNAL/TOPICS/EXTHEALTHNUTRITIONANDPOPULATION/EXTHIVAIDS/ 0,,contentMDK:20740254~menuPK:376477~pagePK:64020865~piPK:149114~theSitePK:376471,00.html

CHAPTER 5:
INCLUSIVE EDUCATION IN NORTHERN IRELAND AND SOUTH AFRICA
~ A CONVERSATION

JACKIE LAMBE, UNIVERSITY OF ULSTER

NITHI MUTHUKRISHNA, UNIVERSITY OF KWAZULU NATAL

JABULANI NGCOBO, UNIVERSITY OF KWAZULU NATAL

NITHI MUTHUKRISHNA is professor in the School of Education and Development, University of KwaZulu-Natal, Pietermaritzburg campus, South Africa. Her research and teaching interests are in the areas of policy and practice related to social inclusion and exclusion, education for social justice and equity, and the psychology of learning and teaching, with a particular focus on child health and well-being.

In 1995, she served as a member of the national Review Committee on the Organisation, Governance and Funding of Schools (Hunter Commission) (1995) – a process that culminated in the South African Schools Act of 1996. She was member of the National Commission on Special Needs in Education and Training, 1996-1997.

JABULANI NGCOBO is a masters student in the School of Education and Development, University of KwaZulu-Natal, Pietermaritzburg campus. He is currently deputy principal at a rural primary school in Estcourt, province of Kwazulu-Natal. In 2000-2003, he served as coordinator for a Department of Education national pilot project aimed at implementing Education White paper 6: Special education - Building an inclusive education and training system (July 2001).

INTRODUCTION

While very different in size (Northern Ireland is not much bigger than a large game reserve in South Africa), both countries have experienced a long history of political and social struggle. Inclusion, in the broadest meaning of the word, is central to the education policy of both countries.

To explore issues relating to inclusion and inclusive practices this chapter is written by way of a reflective conversation between three educationalists, one from Northern Ireland and two from South Africa. The purpose of the conversation was to gain a clearer understanding of what inclusion might mean in the context of each country.

THE COMPLEXITIES OF INCLUSIVE EDUCATION AND THE DIFFICULTIES IN FINDING A COMMON DEFINITION

NORTHERN IRELAND

In the UK one of the key findings of a Department for Education and Employment (DfEE) report on effective practice in inclusion was to identify confusion among stakeholders over what inclusion actually means. Generally it was seen as moving students from special to mainstream schools. More recently the QCA report on research to investigate curriculum, assessment and qualifications in inclusive learning (2004) found that the statement on inclusion from the National Curriculum was associated mainly with special educational needs (SEN) provision with few realising it has far wider implications for other marginalized groups of learners. The same report found that while the goals of the inclusion chapter were laudable, the lack of guidance and training on inclusion made it impossible to fulfil the provision satisfactorily.

Commitment to fully inclusive education could perhaps lead to the dismantling of special schools so that the majority of resources and support would be directed towards mainstream schools. Certainly there is a clear message contained within the Special Education and Disability Act (SENDA) that mainstream education can only be refused against parental wishes where the child's inclusion would be incompatible with the efficient education of other children. It states clearly that the term 'other children' refers to those in direct contact on a regular day-to-day basis, with mainstreaming clearly seen as the preferred option for the majority of pupils. Those who support fully inclusive schooling take the view that there is a present tendency within education to focus on the 'normalisation' (Vlachou, 2004) of the individual within existing systems and, therefore, avoiding the challenge of re-evaluating the systems themselves. What then is the purpose of inclusive education in the context of the UK (including Northern Ireland)? Is it to integrate SEN pupils using new methods, or might it be to recast education from the ground up? (Pugach, 1995). The former could be considered an additive model of inclusion, encouraging change from within already confirmed SEN practice. This would be instantly recognisable within present school environments in Northern Ireland where modification and adaptation of the existing curriculum is used to accommodate difference. In contrast, however, Pugach presents a generative model as a means of transforming thinking on inclusion. This would necessitate curriculum re-design in a much more complex and extensive way. Schools would not simply point to their inclusion policy as evidence of change. Instead inclusion would be seen as part of a total re-think as to what it means to educate all children in parallel with coordinated curriculum and social reform.

Northern Ireland's academic selection at eleven results in issues relating to inclusive schooling, as the principles of inclusion are at odds with such a system. It has, however, served some of the population very well, with more students with qualifications at the top end of the achievement scale than in England. Nevertheless, at the other end of the scale, the average performance of pupils is lower in Northern Ireland than in England and, in the Programme for International Student Assessment (PISA) which assessed the ability of 15-year-olds from 32 countries, the gap between the highest and lowest scores in Northern Ireland was amongst the widest of those participating. Many changes now taking place in Northern Ireland are aimed at making education more inclusive. While academic selection will end in 2008, much work has yet to be done to ensure successful implementation of whatever new system is finally adopted. Many teachers and parents are concerned as to what the schools of the future will look like. Uncertainty has created lobby groups, some still strongly supporting the continuation of selection and others urging the immediate adoption of inclusive schools.

Inclusion has now become one of the most pressing educational issues both nationally and internationally. Prior to the Education (Northern Ireland) Reform Order (1989), children with a variety of special educational needs were likely to have been taught in special schools. Today many of these children are now educated within mainstream schools and the majority of these pupils (70%) are taught in the non-selective school sector. Schools with larger numbers of pupils with special educational needs may have a learning support class or special unit within the school where some pupils are taught on a full-time basis and others with re-integration as far as possible into regular classrooms. While hardly in keeping with the spirit of inclusive schooling, this has been the main mode of response to date.

South Africa

Since 1994, South African governments have been committed to establishing a society based on democratic values, social justice, and fundamental human rights. The *Constitution of the Republic of South Africa Act 108* of 1996 is considered to be one of the most progressive constitutions in the world and is founded on the fundamental values of equality, human dignity, freedom and social rights of all citizens. The Bill of Rights protects the right of all learners, irrespective of race, gender, sex, pregnancy, marital status, ethnic or social origin, age, sexual orientation, disability, religion, conscience, belief, culture, language and birth, to basic education and equal access to educational institutions. All education legislation and policies that emerged since 1994 are founded on the values enshrined in the Constitution, and commit to provision of quality education for all learners regardless of difference (for example, see the following all published by the Department of Education: *White Paper on Education and Training* of 1995; *South African Schools Act* of 1996; *White Paper on an Integrated National Disability Strategy* of 1997; *Education White Paper 6: Special Needs Education: Building an Inclusive Education and Training System* of 2001; *Education White paper 5 on Early Childhood Education*, 2001).

The concept 'inclusion' emerged in South Africa from progressive critiques of special needs education. Such critiques of special needs education have pointed out the limited and medical discourse of special needs education and have argued that the issue of disability must be located, alongside all forms of oppression, within a human rights framework. Inclusion must be viewed as an 'agenda item' that reflects fundamentals of an equitable and just society (*cf. Report of the National Commission on Special Needs in Education and Training* (NCSNET) and *Training and the National Commission on Education Support Services* (NCESS), November 1997).

Such thinking reflects a shift in the inclusion debate from concerns with supporting the rights of learners with impairments, as has been the focus in the majority of countries of the North, to a focus on all children vulnerable to exclusion and to exclusionary pressures within society. These would include children who do not go to school; those who have access to schooling, but experience barriers to participation; those who live in conditions of poverty, children living with HIV/AIDS, socio-cultural isolation, geographic isolation, racial and/or gender bias; those who live with the burdens of disability and disease, sexual exploitation, family breakdown, unemployment, criminal environments, forced involvement in civil and military conflict, exploitative labour, and limited life chances. Inclusion is seen as seen as one facet of a web of social and human rights violations that a significant proportion of children in South Africa experience.

Education White Paper 6 (Department of Education, 2001) largely reflects this paradigm shift to a broad version of inclusion. White Paper 6 is located within the principles and values of the Constitutional framework of the country. The document embraces the rights discourse underpinning the policy changes in education since 1994. In its conceptualisation of inclusion, the Education White Paper uses the term *"barriers to learning and participation"* – and stresses the need to minimise barriers and maximise participation of all learners. Key barriers in the South African context that render a large number of children and adults vulnerable to learning breakdown and sustained exclusion include: problems in the provision and organisation of education; socio-economic barriers; factors that place learners at risk, such as high levels of poverty, violence and crime, HIV/AIDS epidemic; substance abuse; attitudes; an inflexible curriculum; problems with language and communication; inaccessible and unsafe built environment; inappropriate and inadequate provision of support services to schools, parents, care-givers, families and communities; lack of enabling and protective legislation; disability; lack of human resource development; and lack of parental recognition and involvement.

This more expansive view of social exclusion implies the need to focus on whole communities in which children are suffering multiple deprivation, and agencies are expected to work holistically to tackle problems. It stresses a shift of emphasis away from the assessment, categorisation and educational placement of learners according to their disabilities, towards an engagement with how the system can be responsive to educational difficulties. The concern is not only with a small group of learners categorised as 'disabled', but with an engagement with a wider group of students who are vulnerable to learning breakdown.

Debates in South Africa have also drawn attention to the view that inclusion and exclusion are not simply bipolar concepts. Inclusion is not the binary opposite of exclusion, and that inclusion will not overcome exclusion and evidence of exclusion will always be found in practices of inclusion. Questions arise about what the included have become included in, on whose terms, and how the act of inclusion can produce new exclusions.

WHAT ARE THE CONTRADICTIONS BETWEEN POLICY AND PRACTICE?

NORTHERN IRELAND

Often at the heart of any debate about inclusion is a power struggle about who should have the largest proportion of resources that the system has to offer. In Northern Ireland approximately 30% of learners attend an academically selective school. In theory this choice appears meritocratic while not necessarily inclusive. The Department of Education in Northern Ireland has not yet offered a clear definition of what inclusion will mean for the education system in the province when academic selection is set aside in 2008. It seems strange however that the present system could see itself as inclusive when it 'creams off' 30% of learners into what is a very privileged and better-funded environment - the grammar schools. Such an arrangement sends the message that inclusion is all very well for everyone else (70% of learners), but not for those who score well in two one hour written tests completed at the age of eleven. Furthermore, critics of academic selection have cited social bias in favour of the middle class, the distortion of the curriculum, the inherent stress placed on very young learners, the increase in the level of 'coaching' and the sense of failure and stigma felt by those who fail, as good reasons for its removal (Carlin 2003, Gallagher and Smith 2000).

While the process of academic selection is to be removed in 2008 there has not been uniform approval for this. Many of the population agree that testing learners at 11 in such a cold blooded way is actually detrimental to good educational principles. However, there are many lobby groups who are actively fighting to save academic selection as the preferred model. These groups represent what might be called 'the grammar school' lobby. Cynically one could suggest that those who have attended grammar schools gained most from this privileged experience and are generally likely to be currently in positions of influence. Of course there is always the fear of the new, and within the Northern Ireland population a notion has evolved that we have the 'best' system in the UK, based only of course on the results of the top 30%. We have been much slower to acknowledge the lack of success amongst the rest of the learner population. These students are more likely to be drawn from communities whose members hold less powerful positions in society. Slow adoption of change is not uncommon for countries like Northern Ireland emerging from long periods of political and social struggle. While the histories of Northern Ireland and South Africa are quite different, there appears to be within beleaguered nations, one aspect that is common to all. The behaviour of any such state, whether the power is held by Afrikaners in South Africa or Unionists as in Northern Ireland, shows one particular similarity. They tend to be highly conservative regimes that are rigid in clinging to known practices (Leach, 1989:150). Outside influences are likely to be viewed with suspicion, while change of any kind, tends to be resisted. The end of the apartheid system in South Africa opened the door to international influence that had been long resisted and with it came the move towards inclusive education. In Northern Ireland the conflict affected an end to many years of what could be considered self-government (as far as education was concerned) and a return of these powers to the parliament at Westminster. This, and the influence of wider European law, has helped create a 'change culture' within education that had not previously existed.

For many years the population of Northern Ireland has remained overwhelmingly indigenous and unable to grow into a more multi-cultural society as other parts of the UK have done. The troubled situation tended to inhibit international visitors, and to offer less incentive to the possibility of encouraging economic migrants than other areas.

With a more peaceful and stable society, this is changing and there has been a steady growth in the population of those from a wider range of cultural and racial backgrounds than ever before. At the beginning of the 21st century the Chinese community are now the largest minority ethnic group in Northern Ireland. Currently there are more people in Northern Ireland who use Cantonese as their first language than those who claim Irish as theirs. This also presents challenges for the education system as it moves towards inclusive schooling.

SOUTH AFRICA

South Africa still faces major challenges in building an inclusive education system and in making a clean break with the legacy of the apartheid past, despite the policy and legislation in place aimed at redressing the imbalances and injustices of the past. The history of education in South Africa reflects massive deprivation and lack of provision for the majority of people. These inequities can be directly attributed to social, economic and political factors that featured in the history of South African society during the years of apartheid. In South Africa, the notion of social exclusion, therefore, includes poverty. Although South Africa has undergone dramatic social, political and economic transition in the last decade, the dynamics of the apartheid era continue to reproduce poverty and inequality. The majority of South African citizens experience either extreme poverty, or continued vulnerability to becoming poor. Poverty is clearly the most pervasive exclusionary factor in society. There is broad agreement that some 40-50% of people in South Africa can be categorised as being poor (May, 2000).

There has been growing scepticism regarding education policy implementation in South Africa, including *Education White Paper 6*, with critics claiming that, while much has been done to formulate policies, little has been accomplished in transforming the education system. A key issue in debates is that South Africa's macro economic policy over the last decade has had significant effects on education. Criticisms have been raised that focus has been on achieving macro-economic targets at the expense of equity and redress. It has become evident that the structure of the economy in South Africa has not necessarily worked to facilitate the government's commitment to human rights and equity for all its people. Since 1994, the government recognised that a sustained improvement in the country's macro-economic performance was necessity for successful socio-economic transition. Strengthening the economy based on the principle of growth through redistribution was one of the key foundations of the government until 1996.

However, by the end of 1996, this transformational policy was gradually withdrawn. The discourse has shifted from an emphasis on redress to fiscal restraint and privatisation of state assets even in the face of mass unemployment. In its place, the government released the Growth, Employment and Redistribution Strategy (GEAR) – a neo-liberal macro-economic programme of deregulation, privatisation and fiscal restraint. The economy of neo-liberalism embedded in GEAR is the belief in an unfettered free market system, which stems from the political ideology that the state should not interfere or intervene in individual lives.

The government argued that GEAR was necessary for participation in the economic framework imposed by globalisation, and the impact of global conditions on national economies (Mokate, 2000). Fiske and Ladd (2004) argue that this conservative shift in economic policy was largely motivated by the desire to convince international investors that the new South Africa could manage its fiscal affairs in a responsible manner. This combination of fiscal austerity and the economic slow down constrained additional public spending of any type.

The amounts allocated to social services, including education, were inadequate for the degree of social redress, inequality and imbalances that exist. The upshot of this is that promotion of the market enhances social, gender, racial, and regional inequality rather than combating it.

The neo-liberal economic policies adopted by the South African government since 1996 have not so far been successful even in its own terms. GEAR is posited on the assumption that high levels of growth are supposed to provide the resources to address inequity. However, the expected new foreign investment did not materialise at the rate expected – the result was a significant decline in economic growth. In line with neo-liberal economics, fiscal discipline became a more significant priority than social provision and equality enhancement.

This has made it extremely difficult to address social backlogs in health, education and welfare, amongst others. The challenge in education is the implementation of policy that will bring about equity in schooling in the face of budgetary constraints, and contextual realities such as inadequate teacher development programmes, lack of resources, poverty and underdevelopment and lack of capacity in provincial education departments. Pilot projects aimed at implementing *Education White paper 6*, largely managed by the NGO sector or outside service providers, have not been sustainable (Perumanl, 2005; Pather, 2004).

What questions are central to debates on inclusive education?

Northern Ireland

Northern Ireland is a small region within the UK (approximately 1.5 million people). However, because we are part of the UK we have enjoyed the financial support this provides. As part of the EU we have also benefited from extra financial support over a sustained period because of the troubled situation. The infrastructure has been 'propped up' by this over the years so that we have enjoyed the same health, education and welfare benefits as the rest of the UK regions. Over the past 30 years, however, civil unrest has been a costly drain on resources. Terrorist targets were often focused on business and industry suffered a great deal during this time. While Northern Ireland considers itself a rural or farming economy, historically industry in the province was based in textiles and shipbuilding, which have both almost disappeared in face of competition from developing countries. Most of the present employment today is based on the service industry and a large percentage of the population work for government administration bodies; for example, the University of Ulster is the third biggest employer in the province. Northern Ireland is not considered a wealth-creating region and is, in fact, dependant on UK and EU financial support.

Northern Ireland is tied strongly to UK and the EU laws and legislation, including recent laws that relate to inclusion (Disability Discrimination Act, Special Educational Needs and Disabilities Act) and is legally bound to uphold these. Certainly there have been clear changes in the last few years. At one time, for example, learners who had physical disabilities had no entitlement to access mainstream schools. Even if the learner was deemed to be intellectually capable of an academic education access could be denied. This is unlikely to happen today, especially as parents are now much more aware of their legal rights. One of the contradictions of inclusive policy and practice has been found in the drive to mainstream all learners. Unless the supporting infrastructure is in place (e.g. finance, resourcing, staffing) there have been problems arising. Some parents, for example, have complained that instead of feeling included, learners with special needs can in fact feel very isolated within a mainstream setting. While policy and legislation may enforce equality of access to educational opportunities for all, it is more problematic to ensure attitudes of acceptance and tolerance amongst educators. This has been one of the perceived problems of an inclusion policy that has not actually won the hearts and minds of those at the front line of the educational system.

South Africa

There has been rich debate in more recent years on the nature of the concepts of inclusion/exclusion and its usefulness to the South (Porteus, 2003; Sayed, 2002; Muthukrishna and Sader, 2004). It has been argued that debates around the issue of inclusion/exclusion are intensely political and part of political questions about the nature of society, and the status afforded to people in varying forms and structures of social organisations. Inclusion is about questions of access for all people. The issue is about who is in and who is out, and about which students are valued in the educational mainstream and who are relegated to the status of 'other'.

One argument has been that a discussion of social inclusion and exclusion cannot be divorced from inclusion and exclusion in society. Many of these debates have interrogated the concepts of social inclusion and exclusion from an equity and human rights framework. Social exclusion is seen as a process of long term non-participation in any social, political, economic systems that integrate the society in which the individual resides.

Social exclusion occurs *in context* – in the complex conditions and factors that prevent a child from participating in schools, communities and society. The importance of the need to investigate the nature of social injustices at a deep societal and institutional level is emphasised. In other words, in order to address social exclusion there is a need to focus on wider contextual factors, and on the deep structural socio-economic conditions and relations of society which maintain exclusionary practices.

Many of the debates emanate from the view that education policy and practice does not just involve schools, classrooms and curricula activities, but interacts with economic, social, and political relations, and various social structures, social relations and processes. Central to this analysis are issues of power and conflict. For example, desegregation of formerly white, Indian and coloured schools has provided access to all, but has resulted in the inclusion of only a minority of African children. It has resulted in the distinct re-alignment of socio-economic groups that is taking place in schools. A large-scale exodus of middle class black, coloured and Indian parents into state, private and semi-private formerly white schools has taken place. These are economically better resourced schools, leaving other schools largely with the poorest members of the community.

The pattern of desegregation shows movement of African learners into English speaking white, Indian and coloured schools. There is no movement towards African schools, that is, in the opposite direction (Soudien, 2004). In addition, the dominant mode of racial integration has been assimilation into the dominant culture and ethos, rather than an anti-racist approach. Children are offered the values and practices of middle-class schools, which officially promote non-racialism and gender equity, but in practice are far from gender sensitive and race blind. So assimilation is hegemonic as a practice of integration in schools.

Debates have recognised the highly complex nature in which race, class, gender and other categories intersect and inter-relate and result in unique individual and group experiences in South Africa. For example, it has been recognised that social class is a critical component of the reconfigured education system. Although education policy was intended to reconcile the interests of competing and unequal social classes and races, a new deracialised middle class has emerged. A criticism that has emerged is that while education policy has been targeted at improving provision for the poor, it has protected public schools for the middle class. For example, a private and semi-private school sector has emerged and grown since 1994.

Decentralisation has democratised local control of schools in that authority and governance of schools are devolved to schools, and parents have the responsibility for their children's schools. However, what this has done is given the middle class the greatest command over how their schools are run, rights to admission, what school fees are set and who has power on governing bodies, and there is evidence of subtle ways in which access and inclusion are regulated. High fees set by parents in many schools count against poor parents (for example, children of domestic workers) even though they have a statutory right to admission according to the South African Schools Act of 1996. Schools require poor parents to apply for fee exemption, which in reality is a complicated process which leads to stigmatisation. Despite *Education White Paper 6*, special education still exists as an elaborate second system which serves a small minority of learners. This fragmented educational bureaucracy continues to exclude and marginalise these learners from the mainstream of education provision through labelling disabled learners and separating them from their peers in mainstream schools.

Provision remains largely inadequate in terms of services and resources for African disabled children, particularly in rural areas. Due to the formerly racially segregated history of education in South Africa, such provision is either grossly lacking or non-existent.

Education White Paper 6: Special Needs Education (Department of Education, 2001) has legislated that placement in mainstream schools be an option for children with disabilities. This is accurately captured in the following clause:

> "In an inclusive education and training system, a wider spread of educational support services will be created in line with what learners with disabilities require. This means that learners who require low-intensive support will receive this in ordinary schools and those requiring moderate support will receive this in full-service schools. Learners who require high-intensive educational support will continue to receive such support in special schools." (Department of Education, 2001:1.3.7)

There is a mismatch between policy and practice as many disabled children still remain excluded from formal education (many of them still in community-run day-care centres without appropriate educational provision), and teachers often respond negatively to the inclusion of a disabled child in the classroom so that disabled learners are not valued in the school environment. This is an indication of the fact that educational change is not simply a matter of redrafting legislation and restructuring services. The complexity of educational reform requires a more systematic and considered approach to the process of implementing change which targets both the culture and processes of organisational arrangements.

CURRENT PRACTICES - SOME OBSERVATIONS
NORTHERN IRELAND

In December 2006 I was visiting a post-primary school in Northern Ireland with the view to observing a student teacher on her teaching practice placement. This is an important part of my role as a Programme Director for a Post-graduate Certificate in Education at the University of Ulster and, because I spend so much of my time in schools, I would consider myself to be familiar with current schools practices generally. I was waiting in the school foyer to be collected by the student teacher who I was there to observe. Sitting beside me were two pupils aged about fourteen from the school who were engaged in conversation. The conversation was not whispered and it was impossible for me not to overhear. Here is a general outline of how their words flowed.

Girl to boy:	*Did you get a good part in the school show this year?*
Boy	*Yes it's big part though not as big as the one I got last year.*
Girl	*I thought you would have got the lead.*
Boy	*I should have … but well … you know …* **her** *son got it.*

A knowing nod of acknowledgement went between them at this point and I struggled to stifle a smile as I realised that the '*her*' in question was probably the teacher directing the school show.

Girl	*Huh! That's typical … it's the same every year! You are a far better singer than he is. I don't think it's fair.*
Boy	*I know I am.* (He said with all the arrogance of youth.) *Anyway I've still got a big part, so that's the main thing.*

Just at that moment another female pupil rounded the corner and interrupted their conversation, whispering something almost conspiratorial into the boy's ear. He immediately pulled a face reminiscent of someone who has just been gripped with a sharp pain and responded with a loud guffaw. This had the affect of sending the girl who had interrupted into a fit of hysterical laughter before she retired back around the corner she had appeared from.

Girl (1)	*What did she want?*
Boy	*Doesn't matter!* (the boy said sheepishly)
Girl	*I bet I know! Was she telling you that* (a girl's name) *was telling everyone in school that she's your girlfriend?*
Boy	*Yes! How did you know that?*
Girl	*She's been telling everyone … didn't you know?*
Boy	(Sigh) *I'm fed up with her! She won't leave me alone, she's always sending me notes or getting some of her friends to tell me how much she wants to go out with me! My girlfriend is going mad about it and says if she doesn't stop she's going to beat her up!*
Girl	*I don't blame her. If she was after my boyfriend, I'd do the same!*

At this point the conversation was brought to a sudden halt by the arrival of two adult members of staff who took each pupil away in different directions.

I smiled to myself first because of the ordinariness of the conversation and by the fact that the two young people were impervious to my presence. There were other factors in what I had just witnessed that also made me sit up and think. What I omitted from my description was the fact that both these young people were quite severely disabled. I was later told that both pupils suffer from cerebral palsy and use walking frames. The boy in particular had speech impediments that made understanding his conversation quite a challenge. The adults who came to take them to class were clearly assistants assigned to provide learning support for each child. This was a mainstream post-primary school and yet here were two young people who, despite having very specific special educational needs, seemed (certainly by their demeanour and conversation) to see themselves as included. In spite of their disabilities these learners appeared to be comfortable with their surroundings and saw themselves as persons of worth within the school community. I thought back to my own teaching experience. Even a decade ago I am not sure I would have observed the same tableau anywhere in Northern Ireland outside a Special School. Had I just witnessed some evidence that inclusive education was working?

We have spent large sums of capital in promoting inclusive policies, but while policy and legislation may enforce equality of educational opportunities for all in aspects such as physical access, it is more problematic to ensure attitudes of acceptance and tolerance amongst educators.

Studies of both pre-service and in-service teacher attitudes towards inclusion of pupils with Special Educational Needs (SEN) in mainstream classrooms have shown that attitudes were influenced by the amount of education and academic preparation they received. This suggests that improving and increasing training provision at the pre-service phase of teacher education would be the most effective method of promoting better attitudes to inclusion.

SOUTH AFRICA

A recent study by Ngcobo (2006) aimed to listen to how teachers position themselves within socially constructed discourses of disability and inclusion in a mainstream setting that has integrated disabled learners. It further attempted to examine ways in which teachers' constructions of their experiences of inclusion of disabled learners in a semi-rural township context shape their personal lives, beliefs, and practices. In essence, the study sought to analyze the interactional dynamics of inclusion and exclusion. Findings of the study revealed that teachers positioned themselves within discursive limits of dominant discourses. This was evident in how they constructed disabled learners as not meeting some pre-established standard of the discourse of normalcy. There was also evidence of policy-practice tensions in the voices of teachers regarding support provision and delivery of a 'curriculum for all'.

Ngcobo (2006) found that despite having spent more than four years with disabled children, discourses of difference as deficit still emerged in how teachers constructed learner identities. Learners were often constructed as not meeting some pre-established norm or standard of the 'real' child as found in the study by Reay (2004:32). Teachers' narratives revealed that the learner with a disability was receiving the judgement that they were different, marked or inferior. Two of the teachers reported,

> "They [disabled children] are very short-tempered. They are easily irritable … This other boy, Sizwe, he is a bully – he beats others."

> "… most of them [disabled children] are very disruptive. They are disruptive even in the classroom."

Deficit thinking and pathologising the lived experiences of learners shaped teachers' understandings of who should have access to mainstream and special education. These were commonly framed in powerful blaming discourses: constructions of difference, which hold individuals in a 'mechanism of objectification' (Foucault, 1977:187), continued to exist. This constructed disabled learners as individual objects to be "treated", "changed", "improved", "trained or corrected", "normalised". Within this context, teachers' narratives revealed that teachers understood their role as helping disabled learners do ordinary things, in order for them to gain the required amount of social capital, the condition of which was to become 'more like us'. As one teacher expresses the notion:

> "… they can now fit in the mainstream classroom …"

The problematic dimension of this is that if teachers are out to make disabled learners 'more like us', the unique abilities and potentials of learners are likely to be disregarded. Ngcobo points out that this promotes human helplessness as power is stripped from the learner.

Ngcobo suggests that the findings point to the fact that, in essence, the education system does not examine the ideological, political, and economic 'needs' of learners with disability within the context of inclusion. As stressed by Sayed (2002) inclusion and exclusion are not simply bipolar processes. Inclusion in itself presents problems of co-option and control, and does not imply that people are not excluded. Creating inclusive schools and communities requires an understanding of the multiple intersecting and interlocking influences, for example, the micropolitical and micro-cultural conditions in schools and their communities; the politics of participation of education department officials; teacher identities, the extent of human and social capital; the macroeconomic policy of the state, and other competing policies.

SOME CONCLUDING THOUGHTS

The term 'inclusion' is a 'keystone' (Booth *et al*, 2000) of government policy not just for education in the UK, but internationally. However, it is also clear that the vision of what inclusive education really means depends strongly on the context to which it is applied.

Visiting South Africa allowed the present teacher educator to gain some understanding of the constitutional vision as well as the difficulties presented in meeting such a vision in the context of a developing country. I sensed that the constitutional vision was aligned in many ways to the Pugach view of re-constructing education from the ground up. I also recognised the constraints placed on re-construction are clearly associated with issues relating to economics, health, poverty, a long history of a system that was designed to foster racial hatred and, of course, the need to ensure that a huge and diverse population are willing and able 'buy into the vision'. In Northern Ireland we do not have a single, written constitution, possibly because we would be unlikely to find sufficient areas on which we agree. Words, like symbols, in Northern Ireland can take on diverse meaning depending on the politics of the individual. However, we are subject to European led directives and legislation on inclusion and generally comply with these. We have spent a great deal of money on education in the last two decades and there are plans to reconstruct the traditional academic selection model with a much more inclusive one. We may have had the finance to re-shape educational policy, but have we had the will? Because we have not yet decided on how the new model will look, it is likely that there may still be a significant number of educators who see inclusion as relating to the integration of learners with SEN rather than in its broader definition. In effect, there is still a battle ahead to win hearts and minds.

For those involved in Initial Teacher Education there is a recognition that it is here that positive attitudes towards inclusive education must start, and I conclude by offering some suggestions as to employing what might be a more aggressive approach.

- First, there is a need to provide within the ITE teaching programme time and activities that allow student teachers to deconstruct the term 'inclusion' in context so that they develop a broader perspective.

- Second, they need opportunities to experience teaching in an environment that has embraced this broader vision and is not just complying or paying lip service to government directives.

REFERENCES

Ainscow, M., Farrell, P. and Tweddle, D. (2000) Developing Policies for Inclusive Education: a study of the role of local education authorities. *International Journal of Inclusive Education,* 4, (3) pp211-229.

Aramidis, E. and Norwich, B. (2002) Teachers' attitudes towards integration/inclusion: a review of the literature. *European Journal of Special Needs Education,* 17 (2) pp129-147.

Booth, T., Ainscow, M., Black-Hawkins, K., Vaughn, M. and Shaw, L. (2000) *Index for Inclusion: Developing Learning and Participation in Schools.* Bristol: Centre for Studies in Inclusive Education.

Carlin, J. (2003) 'The Northern Ireland selective system: a wind of change'. *The Irish Journal of Education,* 24, pp70-79.

Constitution of the Republic of South Africa (Act 108 of 1996) http://www.info.gov.za/constitution/1996/96cons.htm.

Department of Education (2001) *Education White Paper 6: Special Education: Building an inclusive education and training system.* Pretoria: Department of Education.

Department of Education (1995) *White Paper on Education and Training.* Pretoria: Department of Education.

Department of Education (1997) *Report of the National Commission on Special needs in Education and Training (NCSNET) and the National Committee on Education Support Services (NCESS).* Pretoria: Department of Education.

Department of Education (2004) *Future Post-primary arrangements in Northern Ireland. Advice from the Post-Primary Working Group* (The Costello Report). Bangor: Department of Education.

Department of Education (2001) *Education for the 21st Century; report by the Post-Primary Review Body* (The Burns Report). Bangor: Department of Education.

Department for Education and Skills (2004) *Removing Barriers to Achievement. The Government's Strategy for SEN.* London: Department for Education and Skills.

Fiske, E. and Ladd, H. (2004) Balancing private and public resources for basic education: school fees in post apartheid South Africa *in* L. Chisholm (ed), *Changing class: Education and social change in post apartheid South Africa* (pp.57-88). Cape Town: Human Sciences Research Council.

Foucault, M. (1977) *Discipline and Punish: The birth of the prison.* Harmondsworth: Penguin.

Gallagher, T. and Smith, A. (2000) *The effects of the selective system of secondary education in Northern Ireland.* Research papers Vols. 1 and 2. Bangor: Department of Education for Northern Ireland.

Howell, C. (2003) *A critical analysis of Education White Paper 6.* Unpublished manuscript. Bellville, Cape Town: Education Policy Unit, University of Western Cape.

Lambe, J. and Bones, R. (in press) 'Student teachers' attitudes to inclusion: implications for Initial Teacher Education in Northern Ireland', *International Journal of Inclusive Education.*

Leach, G. (1989) *The Afrikaners – their last Great Trek.* Johannesburg: Southern Book Publishers.

May, J. (2000) Growth, development, poverty and inequality *in* May, J. (ed) *Poverty and Inequality in South Africa: Meeting the challenge.* Cape Town: David Phillip Publishers, pp1-18.

Mokate, R. (2000) Macro-economic context *in* May J. (ed) *Poverty and inequality in South Africa: meeting the challenge.* Cape Town: David Phillip, pp.51-73.

Muthukrishna, N. and Sader, S. (2004) Social Capital and the Development of Inclusive Schools and Communities. *Perspectives in Education,* 22(1), pp17-26.

Ngcobo, E. J. (2006) *How do teachers position themselves within socially constructed discourses of disability and inclusion? A case study at a semi-rural township school in KwaZulu Natal.* Draft unpublished manuscript. Pietermaritzburg: School of Education and Development, University of KwaZulu Natal.

Office of the Deputy President (1997) *White Paper on an Integrated National Disability Strategy.* Pretoria: Government Printer.

Pather, S. (2004) *Understanding sustainable inclusive education development: Lessons from a schools and its communities in rural South Africa*, unpublished doctoral dissertation. Canterbury Christchurch University College, University of Kent.

Perumal, J. (2005) *Towards inclusive education: Exploring policy, context and change through an ethnographic study in a rural context in KwaZulu Natal.* Unpublished doctoral dissertation. University of KwaZulu Natal, Durban: Faculty of Education.

Porteus, K. (2004) The state of play in early childhood development *in* L. Chisholm (ed) *Changing class: Education and social change in post apartheid South Africa* (pp339-366). Cape Town: Human Sciences Research Council.

Pughach, C. M. (1995) On the Failure of Imagination in Inclusive Schooling. *Journal of Special Education,* 29, pp212-223.

Reay, D. (2004) Finding or losing yourself? Working class relationships to education *in* Ball, S. J. (ed) *Sociology of education.* London: RoutledgeFalmer.

Sayed, Y. (2002) *Exclusion and inclusion in the South with reference to education: a synthesis of the literature.* Unpublished manuscript. University of Sussex, UK: Centre for International Education.

Sayed, Y. (2003) Educational exclusion/inclusion: Some debates and issues. *Perspectives in Education,* 21 (3), pp1-12.

Sayed, Y. and Soudian, C. (2003) (Re)framing educational inclusion/exclusion discourses: Limits and possibilities. *IDS Bulletin,* 34 (1), pp9-20.

Schleicher, A. and Tamassia, C. (2000) *Measuring student knowledge and skills.* PISA Paris: OECD.

Soudian, C. (2004) 'Constituting Class': an analysis of the process of 'integration' in South African schools *in* L. Chisholm (ed) *Changing class: Education and social change in post apartheid South Africa* (pp89-114). Cape Town: Human Sciences Research Council.

Soudian, C. and Sayed, Y. (2004) A new racial state? Exclusion and inclusion in educational policy and practice in South Africa. *Perspectives in Education*, 22 (4) pp101-111.

South African Schools Act of 1996, *The Special Educational Needs and Disabilities Act* (SENDA) (2002) Crown copyright: HMSO.

Vlachou, A. (2004) Education and inclusive policy-making: implications for research and practice. *International Journal of Inclusive Education,* (8), pp3-21.

Wilczenski, F. L. (1991) *Use of 'Attitudes towards mainstreaming scale'. With undergraduate education students.* Paper presented at the annual meeting of the New England Educational Research Organisation, Portsmouth, NH.

CHAPTER 6:

EDUCATION WITH A PURPOSE:

CURRICULAR CHANGE IN SOUTH AFRICA

KAREN TEASDALE, UNIVERSITY OF CENTRAL ENGLAND

INTRODUCTION

"One of the most striking observations during our visit to South Africa is the passion and belief in the education system that is shared by the teachers we meet. They know the purpose of their curriculum; they understand its ideology; they feel ownership of it and they are able to explain why they are teaching it."
(Diary, Durban, August 2005)

South African education is at a turning point now, which, in some ways, is of the magnitude of that of the UK over a century ago, when compulsory schooling was first introduced. The legacy of the apartheid years has been replaced with optimism for the future that sees education as being not only important to the individual, but vital to the nation as a whole. As the South African Minister of Education, Professor S M E Bengu noted:

"Education and training are central activities of our society. They are of vital interest to every family and to the health and prosperity of our national economy."
(Department of Education, 1995:1)

This upbeat rhetoric was not confined to official proclamation. We saw teachers motivated by change, by the chance to do something that could make a difference, and by a cautious optimism. Government 'spin' about making a difference can be met with a jaded response in the UK, but the teachers we met in South Africa felt that the time was right for change to happen, and that this change could make a difference to the pupils in their schools. The national picture is obviously far from the forefront of the minds of teachers on a daily basis, but their enthusiasm came across as a stark contrast to the often browbeaten practitioners in the English setting.

POST-APARTHEID EDUCATIONAL CHANGE

In any description of contemporary contexts in South Africa, history has a big part to play. The legacy of years of apartheid education cannot be overcome overnight. As Le Metais notes:

"... any education system is a combination of the past, the present, and the future."
(Le Metais, 1999:96)

... and in South Africa, the past is never very far away, especially when the education system itself played such an important role in social injustice and reinforcing inequality:

"In the past it has perpetuated race, class, gender and ethnic divisions and has emphasised separateness, rather than common citizenship and nationhood."
(South African Department of Education's Curriculum 2005 – on-line)

To sweep away years of emphasis on 'separateness' was going to involve taking a major leap forward, and so in 1995 the publication of the Education White Paper was a brave attempt to start the process. The White Paper,

"stressed the need for a shift from the traditional aims-and-objectives approach to outcomes-based education. It promoted a vision of: A prosperous, truly united, democratic and internationally competitive country with literate, creative and critical citizens leading productive, self-fulfilled lives in a country free of violence, discrimination and prejudice."
(Department of Education, 2001:4)

The Preamble to the Constitution of the Republic of South Africa (Act 108 of 1996) recognised clearly the role of education in the realisation of its aims to:

- heal the divisions of the past and establish a society based on democratic values, social justice and fundamental human rights;
- improve the quality of life of all citizens and free the potential of each person;
- lay the foundations for a democratic and open society in which government is based on the will of the people and every citizen is equally protected by law; and
- build a united and democratic South Africa able to take its rightful place as a sovereign state in the family of nations.

"The curriculum aims to develop the full potential of each learner as a citizen of a democratic South Africa." (Department of Education, 2001:8)

The impact of the Constitution permeates educational policy and documentation. It is at the heart of the curriculum reform and the changes that have been implemented to redress the inequalities and divisions perpetuated by the education system under Apartheid; it has driven the rebuilding of the educational environments; identified the need for changes in teacher training and has begun to redress the imbalance of resources between and within regions. South Africa's Constitution is heralded as one of the most progressive in the world, as human rights are at the forefront of the country's democratic philosophy. In addition, its length and detail distinguish it from other statutes. It has fourteen chapters and two hundred and forty three statements which specify clearly *"the rights of all people ... and affirms the democratic values of human dignity, equality and freedom."* (Constitution of the Republic of South Africa, Act 108 of 1996)

When the constitution became law seven million copies were distributed across the country in eleven languages to celebrate the process and to demonstrate further that this was, and would remain, a document written by South Africans for South Africans. From taxi drivers to school Principals, the South Africans that we spoke to during our stay in KwaZulu Natal were immensely proud of their constitution and the enormous changes it signified. If South Africa is perceived as a teenager in terms of its democracy, it has learnt from the collective wisdom of its older peers. Perhaps more importantly it has much to teach them.

AN OVERVIEW OF THE DEVELOPMENT OF THE SOUTH AFRICAN NATIONAL CURRICULUM, ADAPTED FROM THE REVISED NATIONAL CURRICULUM STATEMENTS (Department of Education, 2001 pages 1-6)

1994	The National Education and Training Forum began a process of syllabus revision and subject rationalisation to lay the foundations for a single national core syllabus. Racist and insensitive language was removed from existing syllabi.
1995	White Paper on Education and Training South African Qualifications Act (No 58 of 1995)
1996	National Education Policy Act (No 27 of 1996) provided for the development of curriculum design tools to support the outcomes-based approach. The *Lifelong Learning through a National Curriculum Framework* emphasised the need for major changes in the South African education system. It stressed the need for a shift from the traditional aims and objectives approach to outcomes-based education. (OBE)
Sept 1997	The Heads of Education Departments Committee recommended *the Draft Statements of the National Curriculum for Grades R-9* for Ministerial approval. *Draft Statements of the National Curriculum for Grades R-9* approved by the Council of Education Ministers.
Oct 1997	Statements of the National Curriculum for Grades R-9 published (Government Notice 1445).
1998	Curriculum 2005 was introduced into schools.

May 2000	Review Committee to Streamline and Strengthen Curriculum 2005. Recommendations included:
	   • streamlining its design features and simplifying its language;
	   • improving teacher training, learning support materials and province support;
	   • the relaxation of timeframes for implementation.

June 2000	Council of Education Ministers agreed the Statements should be revised.
January 2001	Ministerial Project Committee to Streamline and Strengthen Curriculum 2005. This comprised 150 curriculum developers.
July 2001	The Draft Revised National Curriculum Statement For Grades R-9 (Schools) was released for public consultation.
December 2001	Ministerial Project Committee reconvened to incorporate the recommendations from the public consultations.
2002	The Revised National Curriculum statement published.
2004	Introduction of the revised National Curriculum Statement Grades R-9 (Schools) in the Foundation Stage.
2005	Introduction of the revised National Curriculum Statement Grades R-9 (Schools) in the Intermediate Phase (Grades 4 - 6).
2006	Introduction of the revised National Curriculum Statement Grades R-9 (Schools) in Grade 7.
2007	Proposed introduction of the revised National Curriculum Statement Grades R-9 (Schools) in Grade 8.
2008	Proposed introduction of the revised National Curriculum Statement Grades R-9 (Schools) in Grade 9.

Outcomes-based education

Under Apartheid the curriculum was over-burdened with content, subjects were taught in rote fashion through 'chalk and talk' and discipline was instilled through corporal punishment. There was little opportunity for critical enquiry, active learning, or even pupil discussion. Outcomes-based education (OBE) replaced a rigid system that was teacher centred, exam driven and demanded that learners were passive. Towers explains:

> *"Education that is outcomes-based is a learner-centred, results-oriented system founded on the belief that all individuals can learn."* (1996:19)

He lists four principles that are necessary for its success:

- learning must be clearly identified;

- progress is based on demonstrated achievement;

- multiple instructional and assessment strategies need to be available to meet the needs of each learner;

- adequate time and assistance need to be provided so that each learner can reach their maximum potential.

> (Towers, 1996, cited in Lorenzen, http://www.libraryinstruction.com/obe.html)

Outcomes-based education (OBE) is a learner-centred process which engages learners in problem solving and critical thinking. It is developmental, encompassing what learners learn and what they are able to demonstrate at the end of the learning process. Therefore, both the process and the product are considered equally important. The learning process is driven by the outcomes and content can be adapted to address the needs of the learner to reflect the learner's local environment and society. Therefore, educators are able to interpret what should be taught and how to teach it based on the local factors within which they work. For example:

> *"Grade 7 learners could be asked to observe an insect found in their area and draw what they observe. This activity allows the teacher to assess whether the learners are able to observe a living creature and make a field sketch. The insect that they choose is not important; it is also not necessary for every learner to choose the same insect."*
> (http://www.heinemann.co.za/Schools/TeachingTips/OBE.asp)

Outcomes-based education enables teachers to:

> *"… bring to the surface the local, hidden and silenced knowledge, and everyday realities of learners. Through surfacing this knowledge, hidden and suppressed reservoirs of cultural knowledge come into being that challenge the Eurocentric and rationalist assumptions of school-based knowledge."*
> (Nekwhevhu 2000, Odora-Hoppers 2001, Malcolm 2003, cited in Chisholm, 2005:194)

A national curriculum is fundamentally a political statement that reflects the struggles of opposing groups to have their interest, values, histories and politics dominate the school curriculum. The content of South Africa's National Curriculum was influenced by vocational, environmental and religious lobbies. Teaching unions were powerful players and teachers asserted their interests through subject specific associations. Chisholm concludes that the Revised National Curriculum Statement *"… was ultimately an historical product of its time, representing a particular selection dependent on the multiplicity of players involved in its construction."* (Chisholm, 2005:205)

CURRICULUM 2005

Curriculum 2005 is comprised of eight learning areas: languages, mathematics, natural science, technology, social sciences, arts and culture, life orientation, economic and management sciences.

The values of South Africa's national constitution are intrinsically linked to the critical and developmental outcomes and provide a template for the type of citizen that the South African government wants to nurture.

The Department of Education is explicit in what learners achieve; specifically, they will:

- demonstrate an understanding of the world as a set of related systems by recognising that problem-solving contexts do not exist in isolation;

- communicate effectively using visual, symbolic and/or language skills in various modes;

- work effectively with others as members of a team, group, organisation and community;

- identify and solve problems and make decisions using critical and creative thinking;

- organise and manage themselves and their activities responsibly and effectively;

- use science and technology effectively and critically showing responsibility towards the environment and the health of others;

- collect, analyse, organise and critically evaluate information;

- be culturally and aesthetically sensitive across a range of social contexts;

- participate as responsible citizens in the life of local, national and global communities;

- reflect on and explore a variety of strategies to learn more effectively;

- explore education and career opportunities;

- develop entrepreneurial opportunities.

(Department for Education, 2001:8)

There is a clear vision not just of the learners, but also of the educators who will be:

> "... qualified, competent, dedicated and caring ... mediators of learning, interpreters and designers of Learning Programmes and materials, leaders, administrators and managers, scholars, researchers and lifelong learners, community members, citizens and pastors, assessors and learning area/phase specialists." (Department for Education, 2001:9)

This illustrates a major shift in the responsibilities of educators and the increased expectations placed upon them. Teacher education institutions now face the challenge of training and preparing educators for their new roles and developing the skills needed to operate within a learner-centred, outcomes-based curriculum which promotes critical thinking, problem solving and discussion. Sayed (Chisholm, 2004:257) warns that *"... there is a risk that providers might focus only on teaching methods, and ignore the need to provide trainee teachers with the content knowledge they also require."* In addition, Sayed states that there is a gap between educational policy and classroom practice which presents a further test for teacher education institutions.

The language of the curriculum was at the heart of the debates during the Curriculum 2005 review which aimed to simplify the curriculum and to increase the human rights content within the outcomes-based framework (Chisholm, 2005:169). A new language for education had to be introduced. This was not simply an injection of jargon for the sake of re-branding the curriculum, but an attempt to further sever the ties from the education system's historical role during Apartheid. **So 'pupils' became 'learners', 'teachers' became 'educators' and 'subjects' were replaced by 'learning areas'.** Chisholm explains that *"... the renaming was necessary to signify new approaches and habits of thinking consistent with democracy."* (2002:196)

Furthermore, Chisholm states that changing *"the meanings of words is crucial if their associations with the past or unpleasant experiences are to be broken."* (2002:197).

The Review Committee wanted the language of the curriculum to be accessible and *"relatively free from new assessment driven terminology"* (Chisholm, 2002:197) that was occurring in educational reforms developing in the USA, Australia and New Zealand. As a result the Cabinet resolved in July 2000 that the National Curriculum Statements *"... must deal in clear and simple language with what the curriculum requirements are at various levels and phases."* (Department of Education, 2001:6)

The National Curriculum in England

"In South Africa the restructuring of post- apartheid education involved introducing a system that prepares learners for a role in the new democracy. In England the education for democratic citizenship was introduced to respond to an apparent lack of political awareness and interest, especially amongst younger members of society." (Harber and Serf, 2007)

Memories of my own teacher training are fuelled with the impression that, at the time of its introduction, most viewed the National Curriculum for England and Wales as a control measure and that members of the teaching profession were resentful that they were being told what to teach by the Government. I had no impression that it was met with enthusiasm or that there was a sense of exciting new beginnings and opportunities to transform not just education, but society.

How many classroom practitioners in Britain know the aims of the National Curriculum? For most it is a question of turning to the pages that highlight what has to be taught.

"In the day to day urgency of teaching the given curriculum it is easy to push the 'why' into the background and simply get on with the 'how'." (Capel, Leask and Turner, 2005: 338)

Brighouse refers to the introduction of the National Curriculum in 1989 as a *"major accident"* which has *"ill served our curriculum thinking"* as

"… the purpose, scale, framework and choices for inclusion in the curriculum were inappropriate, inheriting the traditions of a bygone age and repeating the mistakes of the 19th and 20th centuries." (Brighouse, QCA discussion paper)

His comments further highlight the differences in ideology between the two national curriculums and their purposes.

"A curriculum should reflect agreed purposes and aims for education based on present and future needs … in half heartedly embracing the principle of equality of opportunity for all, the secretary of state at the time, Kenneth Baker, declared that this implied that we must provide the same curriculum for everyone."

The National Curriculum for England and Wales did not reflect the needs of British society. In fact,

"Concern about the decline in the standard of education in England and Wales in comparison with that of other countries was the root of the decision to introduce a national curriculum for use in all maintained schools in England and Wales."
(Capel, Leask, and Turner, 2001:347)

The National Curriculum was based on narrow aims and introduced a highly centralised and standardised framework. Teachers had little involvement in the development of the curriculum and it was generally felt that their role would be to deliver what had been handed down from on high (Gillard, 1988).

The Times Educational Supplement described the introduction of the National Curriculum in England as *"… an expression of distrust of teacher and belief that just about every educated person (and all parents) know what teachers should be doing better than the teachers"* (TES, 31 July 1987).

The aims of the National Curriculum were to provide 'a balanced and broadly based' curriculum which:

> "... promotes the spiritual, moral, cultural, mental and physical development of pupils at the school and of society; and prepares such pupils for the opportunities, responsibilities and experiences of adult life." (Education Reform Act, 1988 Chapter 40 1.(2))

However, there was "little justification made for the connection between these aims and the subject curriculum that emerged" (Capel, Leask and Turner, 2005:338). Furthermore, the broad sweeping nature of the aims failed to provide explicit guidance about how they could be addressed and what changes they would bring about.

This golden opportunity to look with fresh eyes and holistically at the nature of what was taught in schools, and how it was taught, was missed. Instead of asking the big questions about the role of education, the type of learner that was envisaged and the skills and knowledge needed by future generations, changes were rushed and piecemeal. **Little thought was given to the changing nature of Britain's society and its place in Europe**. Instead of embracing the increasingly multicultural nature of the population, pupils were served a curriculum diet of the traditional, the English and the dead.

Although consultation was invited between August and September 1987, many were cynical about its timing, which coincided with the main school holidays. Furthermore, there was little difference between the consultation document proposals and the final Act despite 15,000 responses. A staggeringly short thirteen months elapsed between the 1988 Education Reform Act becoming law and schools having to teach the new National Curriculum.

CONCLUSION

In England, the education system has incurred only incremental changes since the Education Reform Act of 1988. We have tinkered around the edges and we do not have the vision or the imperative that faces South Africa. Therefore, if we compare the two education systems we can simplistically identify their purpose as that of education to maintain the status quo (England) and education to create a new society (South Africa). This divide is further emphasised by South Africa's Curriculum 2000 and the new strategies for the 14-19 curriculum in England and Wales which focus on enterprise experiences and work related learning. In South Africa there

> "... is a clear belief that education has an essential and unique political role to play in the transformation of South African society." (Carter, Harber and Serf, 2003:14)

In contrast, Britain's education system has been designed to serve the needs of the economy, the ruling elite and the status quo rather than the needs of society. Because after all, during its initial conception, someone stated that there is no such thing as society.

Key Points

- The South African Constitution is considered to be one of the most progressive because of its stance on human rights, its detail and its length.

- The South African Constitution permeates through education policy and documentation.

- The content-heavy Apartheid curriculum and rote learning have been replaced by an Outcomes-based Education (OBE) and active learning.

- South African teachers have felt part of the educational reform and welcome the new changes. The introduction of the National Curriculum in England and Wales was not received with such positivism and teachers felt that the system was imposed on them.

- The two national curricula serve two different purposes: the National Curriculum for England and Wales serves the needs of the economy whilst the South African National curriculum serves the needs of society.

Signposts

- Chisholm, L. (2004) (ed) *Changing Class: Education and Social Change in Post-Apartheid South Africa*. Cape Town: HSRC Press.

- Chisholm, L. (2005) The making of South Africa's National Curriculum Statement. *Journal of Curriculum Studies*. 37 (2), pp193-208.

- The Revised National Curriculum Statements grades R-9
  http://www.polity.org.za/html/govdocs/policy/2002/curriculum/part1.pdf

- *Constitution of the Republic of South Africa* (Act 108 of 1996)
  http://www.info.gov.za/constitution/1996/96cons.htm

Points for Discussion

- To what extent do you consider the aims of the education system in your role as an educator?

- How can we encourage trainee teachers to question the role of education in developing 'citizens'?

- What lessons can we learn from the South African educational reforms?

REFERENCES

Brighouse, T. *Accidents can happen:* QCA discussion paper http://www.qca.org.uk/11475.html (Accessed on 23 January 2006).

Capel, S., Leask, M., and Turner, T. (2005) *Learning to Teach in the Secondary School.* 4th edition. London: Routledge.

Carter, C., Harber, C. and Serf, J. (2003) *Towards Ubuntu: Critical teacher education for democratic citizenship in South Africa and England.* Birmingham: Development Education Centre.

Chisholm, L. (2005) The making of South Africa's National Curriculum Statement. *Journal of Curriculum Studies,* 37 (2), pp193-208.

Department of Education, (2001) *Revised National Curriculum Statement Grades R-9.* Pretoria: Department of Education.

Constitution of the Republic of South Africa (Act 108 of 1996) http://www.info.gov.za/constitution/1996/96cons.htm (Accessed on 23 January 2006)

Department of Education, (1995) *Education and Training in a democratic South Africa: first steps to develop a new system.* Pretoria: Department of Education.

Harber, C. and Serf, J. (2007) Teacher Education for a Democratic Society. *Teaching and Teacher Education,* 22 (8) forthcoming.

Gillard, D. (1998) *The National Curriculum and the role of the primary teacher in curriculum development.* http://www.dg.dial.pipex.com/educ07.shtml (Accessed on 24 January 2006).

Le Metais, J. (1999) Values and Aims in Curriculum, *in* Moon, B. and Murphy, P. (eds) *Curriculum in Context.* London: Paul Chapman.

Sayed, Y. (2004) The case of Teacher Education in Post Apartheid South Africa: politics and priorities, *in* Chisholm, L., (ed) (2004) *Changing Education and social change in post apartheid South Africa.* Cape Town: HSRC Press.

Towers, J.M. (1996) An elementary school Principal's experience with implementing an outcome- based curriculum. Catalyst for Change, 25 (Winter), pp19-23 *in* Lorenzen, M. *Using Outcome-Based Education in the Planning and Teaching of New Information Technologies.* http://www.libraryinstruction.com/obe.html (Accessed on 5 March 2006).

http://www.heinemann.co.za/Schools/Curriculum2005.asp (Accessed on 23 January 2006).

CHAPTER 7:
LEARNING TO LEAD:
THE POLITICS OF PHYSICAL EDUCATION

HELEN MILES, BIRMINGHAM ADVISORY AND SUPPORT SERVICES

THE CONTRIBUTION OF PHYSICAL EDUCATION TO EDUCATIONAL OUTCOMES

'Physical education' on a school or higher education curriculum has survived almost a century of debate about how well it describes what learners and their teachers experience. The six aspects listed as the content areas in the English National Curriculum have their origins in adult community life and link to cultural events such as theatre, religion, sport, health, exploration, war without weapons, and national celebrations.

Physical education and sport can be manipulated to emphasise the distance between class or cultural or tribal affiliations in the same way as it can be used to bring varying groups of different gender, age and race to experience common identities and collective emotions. Evidence of its importance in the UK, and, it can be argued, in other countries, can be measured by the financial investment, the media interest and the political status of those who carry ministerial responsibilities for it. Its use in the formal education process has been evident in schools that service different groups in the population.

Justifications of its value range from blatant nationalism, to social control, to its value for behaviour management inside and outside school. For example, to keep young people off the streets at night the police in some areas in the UK are using midnight basketball and football activities to keep them engaged. If there is any agreement at all, it is that Physical Education and sport is not neutral - it is a political and commercial activity that may be used for good or bad depending on the intentions of those defining the current agenda.

While all education should be healthy in one sense of the word, physical education alone gives the fitness and skill dimension a health value. It offers many opportunities for pupils to raise their self-esteem, to achieve membership of groups important to them and to be involved substantially in activities regarded as worthwhile by parents, peers, the media and society at large. While fitness is an element regarded as necessary for participation, health can be an outcome of such participation.

With today's political agenda, a strategy that can simultaneously offer to reduce dependency on the health service, improve behaviour on our streets and contribute to national cohesion and pride is made for the 21st century governments. It is also that many young people find it an attractive and fashionable way to express themselves and show their identity.

In England, physical education and school sport is high on the government's agenda. Significant finances have been devoted for the purpose of:

- improving pupil concentration, commitment and self-esteem; leading to higher attendance and better behaviour and attainment;

- improving fitness levels; active children are less likely to be obese and more likely to pursue sporting activities as adults; thereby reducing the likelihood of coronary heart disease, diabetes and some forms of cancer; and

- improving success in international competition by ensuring talented young sports people have a clear pathway to elite sport and competition whatever the circumstances.

(DfES/DCMS, 2002)

In the UK we have inherited substantial benefits for the development of physical education and sport. There is a large body of professionals working at all levels in education and in the political life of the country.

SOUTH AFRICAN DEMOCRATIC CITIZENSHIP AND PHYSICAL EDUCATION

It would be erroneous to ignore the power of the state and the impact policy statements have on how the educational system and society develop in the majority of countries. For example, physical education has been a feature of the debate on the South African vision for democracy. During the apartheid period there was a very divided and unequal education system that prepared young people for the lives they were expected to lead. Major change was needed post apartheid and with this came a shift from traditional curricular aims and objectives to outcomes-based education.

Karl Deventer at the 2nd World Summit on physical education (2005:2) stated that:

> "Certainly physical education is finalised or de-finalised by political interests. But the fragility depends on the balance between several social and political forces. The 'fragile' or 'assured' status of physical education depends upon negotiations conducted in the political trading zone."

This may sound familiar to any physical education or sport leader in educational institutions across the world. Negotiations at the school level, the micro political struggle for time, resources, training and status, have been features of their daily routine. In this way the macro and micro political levels of political trading are as significant in determining reality.

In South Africa the value of sport was officially recognised within the *Manifesto on Values, Education and Democracy* (Ministry of Education, 2001). It highlighted how sport could be used to shape social bonds and nurture nation building in schools. The vision for the new education system is to promote:

> "A prosperous, truly united, democratic and internationally competitive country with literate, creative and critical citizens leading productive, self-fulfilled lives in a country free of violence, discrimination and prejudice." (White Paper on Education and Training, cited in the Overview Revised National Curriculum, 1995:4)

The South African Government recognised that apartheid education had under-rated the importance of physical education and how it can benefit the development of the whole child, and set out to form a policy for Physical Education and School Sport (PESS). Deventer (2005:4) argued that it could:

- aid the promotion of the transformation agenda, particularly the elimination of racism and discrimination in schools and sports activities;

- aid the promotion of organised physical activities as a healthy life-style;

- aid the approach to counter juvenile crime; promiscuity and HIV infection.

However, the Revised National Curriculum (Department for Education, 2002) watered down this view and it is only recently that the profile of PESS has been formally identified. An agreement was signed in March 2005 that identified physical education as one of the focus areas within the Life Orientation curriculum.

Whilst democratic values are now recognised and stated clearly, the challenge remains how to embed these values within the curriculum. The kind of post-apartheid learner envisaged is one who will be imbued with the values and act in the interests of society based on respect for democracy, equality, human dignity, life and social justice (Carter, Harber and Serf, 2003: Ch.3). The government has introduced a new curriculum, which is seen as a curriculum that will instill in our young citizens the values that promote the interests of a society based on respect for democracy, equality, human dignity and social justice. It is envisaged that an outcomes-based curriculum will foster the skills needed for a democratic society in a globalised world (Carter, Harber and Serf 2003: Ch.4). Life Orientation is one of the two new compulsory subjects that have been introduced into the South African school curriculum. Physical education is part of the Life Orientation curriculum and is identified through the learning outcome based on recreation and physical well-being. It is interesting to see that the curriculum here is based on physical development and movement in a very similar way to the English physical education curriculum at present. However, it is a 'top down' model of curriculum development where the vision is disseminated rather than captured as it emerges from everyday practice.

With this focus on physical education in the curriculum how much progress is being made in South Africa? What is the reality? During the study visit we saw schools both in the primary and secondary sector. Schools in South Africa highlight the incredible contrasts within state education sector provision. One school we visited (a former white school) was well resourced and could be compared to a private school in England. It had high quality provision in terms of facilities. This included a swimming pool, gym, dance studio, sports field and hard-court area. Regular out of hours activities were provided, including competitive teams and recreational activities. From discussion with the Principal it appeared the main benefits of physical education were perceived as healthy activity and traditional team sports.

The legacy of apartheid is only too apparent and other schools (historically, and still, black institutions) had very limited resources. In one primary school the sole visible resource was one old-fashioned leather football stuck in a cupboard. However, a range of values placed on physical education were apparent. Some Principals obviously valued physical activity and we watched demonstrations of energetic traditional dancing and a performance by majorettes. I would suggest this is based on the traditional culture of the students, rather than high quality teaching and learning of physical education. At present this post-apartheid legacy, which could be seen as moving from a caste system to a class system, does not entirely allow for the South African vision/philosophy of education to be realised. It was clearly evident that there were tremendous inequalities in terms of resources.

PHYSICAL EDUCATION: VISION IN ENGLAND

England and South Africa both describe themselves as democracies. Harber and Serf state that democracy is a learned behaviour. Education, therefore, has a crucial role to play in developing the characteristics of the type of citizens we want to develop for a democratic society. What does this type of education look like? What do we want young people to be like and to be able to do by the time they leave school? Does physical education support what we are trying to achieve?

> *"Education influences and reflects the values of society, and the kind of society we want to be."* (National Curriculum for England, Key Stages 3 and 4, 2000, QCA website).

Within the values, aims and purpose of the National Curriculum in England there are two specific aims. The second of which appears to be the most relevant to this discussion:

> *"The school curriculum should aim to promote pupils' spiritual, moral, social and cultural development and prepare all pupils for the opportunities, responsibilities and experiences of life."*

The principles that citizenship encompasses are defined implicitly in the English National Curriculum. However, to be taught effectively, they must be enshrined in the ethos of the whole school. Yet schools have to fit into strategies and systems that are developed by government. Recent government documents such as *Every Child Matters*, the Primary strategy: *Excellence and Enjoyment, Transforming Secondary Education* and *Youth Matters* (the Green Paper for Youth), all identify key skills that support the development of democratic citizenship. Central government has been working with local government to undertake a significant change to the way we work with children, young people and their families. The Children Act (2004) sets out new statutory duties and accountabilities for children's services.

The trip to South Africa forced all of us to reflect on our own education system through comparative study. Overwhelmingly we concluded that there was no clear vision for education in the UK. What do we want our young people to be like, to be able to do and to feel like when they leave school? I have also asked many involved in education what they think is the philosophy for education in England. The consistent response has been that they do not know. There is a belief though that the priority for the government, which is promoted in all they do, is about raising standards. This is expressed through league tables and results, which are measured, by exams in limited subject areas only. With regard to physical education there is a clear strategy, but how this links back to an overarching vision for developing a democratic society is debatable.

The Prime Minister launched the Physical Education, School Sport and Club Link (PESSCL) strategy on 2 October 2002. This strategy is being implemented by the Department for Education and Skills (DfES) and the Department for Culture, Media and Sport (DCMS). It is also clear how physical education and sport can support all five outcomes in *Every Child Matters* and many other current education agendas.

Sport Playing its Part (2005:10), a document recently produced by Sport England identifies significant areas where it contributes. For example:

> *"Sport can contribute to the 'making a positive contribution' outcomes of the national framework. It can assist young people to:*
>
> - *engage in decision-making and supporting the community and environment;*
> - *engage in law-abiding and positive behaviour in and out of school;*
> - *develop positive relationships and choose not to bully and discriminate;*

- *develop self-confidence and successfully deal with significant life changes and challenges; and*
- *develop enterprising behaviour."*

The Public Service Agreement target (PSA) set by the Government is a first for physical education and has certainly raised its profile. The Department for Education and Skills (DfES) is surveying all schools annually to review the uptake of physical education and school sport and focuses on the entitlement for all children to have at least two hours high quality physical education and school sport per week. However, a large percentage of schools still reject the importance of physical education and sport or are unable to devote sufficient resources to its development.

MOVING INTO THE 21ST CENTURY

It appears that the present education of young people is mismatched to what they really need to succeed and survive in the 21st century. In physical education, it can be argued that the teaching of the four strands: acquiring and developing skills; selecting and applying skills, tactics and compositional ideas; evaluating and improving performance; and knowledge and understanding of fitness and health, do not have equal focus (QCA, 2004/05). The concentration is on what is acquired and what is developed, and teachers are assessing and testing skills, not pupils' knowledge, understanding, attitudes and involvement in physical education.

In England changes are beginning to take place in educational thinking. The 'Futures Debate' hosted by QCA is encouraging a 'bottom up' not 'top down' approach to curriculum review and reform. It is identifying innovative ways of delivering a curriculum that develops and benefits all young people. There is the growing feeling that the effectiveness of schools cannot continue to be judged purely on attainment based on GCSE results and league tables. Within physical education, QCA is conducting research that identifies how the subject can deliver other aspects of the curriculum and how the impact on the whole school can be assessed. (www.qca/pess.org.uk)

Opening Minds (RSA, 1999) is a report, a project and a philosophy that explores the view that education is becoming increasingly distanced from young people's, and the country's real needs. It suggests that the current information-driven curriculum will not prepare young people for adult life in the 21st century. The concept of *Opening Minds* identifies five categories of competencies that should be developed. They include: competencies for learning; for citizenship; for relating to people; for managing situations; and for managing information.

Schools taking this perspective on board are encouraged to challenge traditional models of curriculum and teaching organisation, and focus the curriculum on developing the competencies and achieving these outcomes.

One school involved in the *Opening Minds* project has identified physical education as a focus for developing the curriculum around the competencies. The curriculum has been revised to link the competencies with the four strands of the physical education National Curriculum referred to above. The school has realised that the competencies easily fit with the existing outcomes they are trying to achieve and are leading this process across the whole school. There appears to be movement away from merely promoting high levels of skills to also promoting key competencies in the current curriculum agenda. A more detailed analysis of how this approach relates to the competency based curriculum in South Africa needs to be examined.

LEARNING TO LEAD: IN SOUTH AFRICA

Leadership is one of the competencies that both the UK and South Africa see as important contributions to developing a democratic society. Physical education and sport can play a huge role as it is about young people learning about themselves and growing in confidence and self esteem. It involves them learning how to work as a team and developing respect for others. Pupils can communicate through physical education and sport across language barriers in ways that other subject areas find difficult. Both South Africa and England have found that using sport and physical education can be valuable as a tool to promote democracy and responsible action by young people. South Africa has recently undergone a major change in physical education as a school subject. It has been replaced by Life Orientation, and has a completely different approach to content and teaching and learning.

Taking responsibility and 'learning to lead' is an element that has been focused on by both South Africa and the UK. During the visit to Durban something that the group considered was the role of sport in education for democratic citizenship. South Africa is involved with *Dreams and Teams* which is a leadership programme based on the English model of *TOP Link*. *TOP Link* is identified as a model to develop active citizenship in the citizenship curriculum for secondary pupils. Both are Youth Sport Trust (YST) programmes that train teachers and educators to encourage and develop leadership skills in young people using the tool of sport. Opportunities are provided for the young leaders to develop citizenship skills through planning and organising junior sports festivals/events. It is the empowerment of individuals to take responsibility and lead something that has an outcome, therefore, supporting 'building democracy.'

The key purpose of the project in South Africa is:

- to develop the creativity and skills of young people through sport leadership;
- to improve cross-cultural understanding among young people;
- to highlight the dreams that young people have for the future, giving them a platform at one of the world's biggest sport events - the 2010 World Cup in South Africa.

At present the British Council in partnership with the YST manages the school link element of *Dreams and Teams*. In the future it may become a module within the Life Orientation part of the curriculum. Schools in South Africa are linked with Specialist Sports Colleges in England and joint training has taken place. The teacher's role is one of overall co-ordinator and facilitator from whom the team seek guidance, advice and support. This is clearly a change of role for staff and students and not something, which takes place easily. From the perspective of a Durban Principal the benefits of *Dreams and Teams* is very clear:

> "This is about everything we stand for - it's about giving our learners the personal and social skills and confidence to really make a difference to our country. Sport is the vehicle, but citizenship is the product. We are already noticing that these learners are taking a more active and confident role on our school councils, and we hope that they will use the skills they have learned to develop sporting activities at school. Fundamentally this is about nation building."

Another comment from an educator stressed how the project has *"… a huge role in bringing races together."* This statement needs to be explored further in terms of whether it was because learners from South Africa and England were brought together through the joint programme with British Council or from inter school relationships/team working. The idea of Curriculum Partnerships is being explored by the YST. They are examining the potential to collectively (that is South Africa and England) find innovative ways in which physical education can be utilised to support the delivery of other curriculum subjects. This in itself has challenges.

Initially the programme developed in England was thought to be easily super-imposed on South Africa. In reality there was no consideration given to the strong racial divisions that exist. This was apparent during the visit where we attended a presentation at a school involved in *Dreams and Teams* and met colleagues from other schools. Comments from staff and the British Council made reference to this fact. It was also interesting to observe the fact that whilst this was about developing student leadership and roles and responsibilities there were no students present at all to give their views. The barbecue we attended afterwards may have been perceived by us as a wonderful opportunity for young leaders to develop management skills. A colleague asked the question at the end of the presentations, *"What was missing?"* students obviously. However, when talking to one of the assistant principals later they highlighted to me why students were not there.

> *"You may wonder why we have no students here at the barbecue. Students would view it, as if they were taking on a subservient role, which re-enforces the culture we are trying to get away from. Blacks serving white people."*

Is this teacher sensitivity or is it reality? Is the culture ready for this change? We know it cannot afford to wait for change to take place and it must be used to support the changing culture that is needed. Included in this, and still to be explored, is whether all students are involved, including both boys and girls.

DO THE GOALS OF TEACHER EDUCATION MATCH THE GOALS OF EDUCATION FOR DEMOCRACY?

An outcomes-based approach to education in South Africa is interactive rather than didactic. Initially the *Dreams and Teams* programme failed because principals and teachers were not fully prepared. They needed to see the value of the programme and not feel that it was something being imposed on them. Principals and teachers are now trained together to ensure they see the relevance and benefits of what they are doing and it is apparent that both groups value the joint training sessions, which helped to break down barriers. They felt it helped build relationships that have been continued back in the school setting.

In the UK *Dreams and Teams* training is for physical education teachers only and continues to be perceived as a project in the majority of schools rather than an approach to teaching and learning. There is a need to influence and gain the support of those in management and leadership positions. However, in the UK *Dreams and Teams* is not embedded in policy and training is primarily of teachers. The approach is seen as physical education, rather than a teaching and learning style and the development of key skills that all pupils should have.

The process for delivering *Dreams and Teams* is based on a facilitation model. This proved to be a significant challenge for educators:

> *"Children are quite fearless … they plunge in … I had to step back and bite my tongue and let them get on with it … they can surprise you".*

> *"It has taught me that pupils can do … they can organise … I am an overseer!"*

were comments made at the meeting in Durban.

At the same time the approach has had a direct impact on teaching. Comments from principals indicated how motivation is low generally amongst educators in South Africa. The programme has re-motivated individuals to give more of their time and work harder. They are using principles from the project in the classroom. As one teacher stated, *"My lessons are now more practical and activity based. I was not doing justice to my students in the past."*

The passion from the schools involved is difficult to quantify. However, from the research YST have undertaken (2005) and from talking to principals and educators during our visit, it is clear there is a strong belief in the skills being developed by students and educators. They see it as support for education for democracy.

> *"I look at Dreams and Teams as part of nation building."* (British Council spokesperson)

> *"We are teaching good citizenship morals for South Africa and helping students to become global citizens."* (Principal)

> **"It instils discipline without imposing it upon them."** (Teacher)

CONCLUSION

Firstly, it is important to examine strategies used to teach and coach, and the quality/capacity of the professionals involved in carrying these strategies forward. The initial and continuous development of teachers and coaches is central to the success of the project. They need to develop the knowledge and understanding that underpins their choice of strategies that:

- promote high levels of skill;
- promote high levels of competencies.

It is clear, also, that an interactive, non-didactic style of teaching is a key to progress. Those who can do this will need to coach those who are training to teach. 'Vision', 'passion', 'support' and 'empowerment' are words that have to be explored fully here.

The type of educators (teachers) that are envisaged within the South African Revised Curriculum are those who are qualified, competent, dedicated and caring. Such educators are perceived as:

> *"mediators of learning, interpreters and designers of Learning Programmes and materials, leaders, administrators and managers, scholars, researchers and lifelong learners, community members, citizens and pastors, assessors and learning area/phase specialists."* (Department of Education Pretoria, 2002:9)

Secondly, educational leaders must reflect on the processes they use to promote the allocation of resources and the dissemination of vision. Their role should focus on auditing the emerging vision of physical education and sport that is being negotiated in every school and to facilitate the establishment of this vision that is emerging from leading practice at grassroots level. Like the teachers who discovered that the pupils had a lot to teach them, those educational managers at Ministerial level will be amazed at the capacities professional adults can bring to their work when empowered to do so. The bidding process may be a useful procedure to link grassroots with decision makers.

KEY POINTS

- To have a vision is a key part of any leadership programme (Fullan, 2001). However, the difficult part may be putting that vision into practice. The other aspects of leadership imposition or consensus, establishing relationships, coaching others or self-improvement frequently limit the grounding of a vision in reality.

- The position in South Africa may be summed up as a country with a clear vision, but where the logistics of its realisation are at an early stage of development and the legacy of apartheid prevents it moving quickly. The position in the UK may be summed up as most logistics are in place, but no consensus about vision is clear.

- Physical education and sport have been used effectively to achieve different educational outcomes for different sections of the population at different times in the last 150 years in the UK. It is certainly not a neutral activity in the political sense. It will be used again to promote the democratic outcomes of education for the 21st century. It can be used effectively in South Africa.

- *Sport Playing its Part* (2005) in the UK traces how sport and physical education can assist young people to get involved in and develop skills of decision making, positive relationships and enterprise – all resulting in changing cultures. Competencies relating to people, managing situations and for citizenship are contributions sport and physical education is already making to the democratic system.

- In South Africa a 'catch up' situation is called for in relation to community and school facilities and resources. It is also essential to speed up the re-skilling of teachers, coaches and administrators. Only if this is successful will there be staff able to negotiate in the macro- and micro-political trading zones. The bidding process may have a significant role to play here.

SIGNPOSTS/FURTHER READING

- Physical Education and School Sport Strategy for England.

- QCA website – Futures curriculum and PESS – www.qca.org.uk/futures.

- David, P. (2005) *Human Rights in Youth Sports*. London: Routledge.

- Department of Education (2002) *Revised National Curriculum Statement Grades R-9 (Schools) Policy*. Pretoria: Department of Education.

- Mourant, A. Democracy for beginners. *Times Educational Supplement*. 25/11/05, p29.

POINTS FOR DISCUSSION

- The importance of political interventions in the change process.

- The relevance of taking a UK model and imposing it on another country (South Africa).

- Where does 'the vision' originate from and how do people take ownership of it?

- How effective will leadership programmes be in encouraging interaction between races in South Africa?

REFERENCES:

Asmal, K. (2002) *A skill-full new curriculum.*
www.southafrica.info/ess_info/sa_glance/education/curriculum.htm

Barker, Y. (2005) *Sport Playing Its Part – The Contribution of Sport to Meeting the Needs of Children and Young People.* London: Sport England.

Carter, C., Harber, C. and Serf, J. (2003) *Towards Ubuntu – critical teacher education for democratic citizenship in South Africa and England.* Birmingham: Development Education Centre.

Department of Education (2002) *Policy Revised National Curriculum Statement Grades R-9 (Schools) Life Orientation.* Pretoria: Department of Education of South Africa.

Department of Education (2002) *Revised National Curriculum Statement Grades R-9 (Schools). Overview.* Pretoria: Department of Education of South Africa.

Deventer, K. (2005) *Physical Education and School Sport: A South African Case Study.* Paper presented at the 2nd World Summit on Physical Education.

DfEE, QCA (1999) *National Curriculum for England, Key Stages 3 and 4.* London: HMSO..

DfEE, QCA (2002) *National Curriculum for Citizenship.* London: HMSO.

DfES, DCMS (2002) *Learning through PE and Sport.* London: HMSO.

Fullan, M. (2001) *Leading in a Culture of Change.* San Francisco: Tom Wiley & Son.

Harber, C. and Serf, J. (2006) Teacher Education for a Democratic Society. *Teaching and Teacher Education*, 22 (8), forthcoming.

Hicks, D. (1999) Visionary Leadership: choosing the future in schools. *Management in Education*, 3 (3).

Ministry of Education (2001) *South African Manifesto on Values, Education and Democracy.* Pretoria: Ministry of Education.

QCA (2006) *Review of National Curriculum Physical Education and School Sport 2004/05.* London: QCA.

RSA (2005) – *The New Curriculum 'Opening Minds'* www.thersa.org/newcurriculum

Times Educational Supplement (2000) *Action speaks louder to teenagers.* London: Times Educational Supplement, 02/06/22.

Chapter 8:
Dreams and Teams:
Changing attitudes – changing lives

Liz Bartley, Ken Stimpson Community School,
Peterborough

Introduction

The *Dreams and Teams* programme is what, in the UK, would be called an Active Citizenship Project, but one which is channelled through the sport area of the curriculum. Its aim is to develop effective leaders and good citizens. The programme was initially a joint development between a number of schools in South Africa, the British Council and the Youth Sports Trust based at Loughborough University, and was based on a pilot project run in the UK in 2003. The model which was developed in the UK could not simply be superimposed into the South African context and, therefore, had to be adapted to fit in with the different cultural, social and political context.

The project enabled groups of young people from the secondary phase to be trained and supported so that they could set up and run sports festivals in local primary schools. Facilitation training took place for staff (including principals) over a five-day period, following which they worked with selected groups of young people to develop their own programmes. By the summer of 2005, 600 young leaders had been trained in 30 schools. The programme has been so successful that now the Department for Sport and Recreation in KwaZulu Natal has delegated a specific budget for the programme to be extended to Junior Schools in the province, and *Dreams and Teams* has been incorporated into the Life Orientation area of the formal curriculum. Further, activities have now been expanded to include areas outside Sport such as Dance, as well as there being a focus throughout the programme on morals and values, and on the characteristics of Young Leaders and their contribution to the community. After each Sports Festival, the young people engage in wider school activities such as Learner Representative Councils (South Africa's version of Student Councils). Achievements are formally recognised on a presentation day.

Impact

As is often the case, the changes which occurred as a result of this project are not easy to quantify. However, at a meeting of head teachers and staff involved in the project which was held at Strelizia School (Durban) it was reported that there were changes in attendance levels, motivation and examination results. However, the following quotations from the teachers at the school give a much better insight into the changes the programme has engendered.

Changes in the school ethos

"The regime change that has taken place in school … it's revolutionary."

"It brought us closer. In the training we were all equal. Our facilitators were educators. At school the hierarchy is always there."

"We feel proud now that we have got leaders."

"Principals spend most of their lives with their head in the swamp. What you forget is you're supposed to pull the plug. The positive is very uplifting."

"Dreams and Teams is transforming principals to realise that they are not the only people in the school who can lead."

AND OF WHAT GOES ON IN THE CLASSROOM

"What we learnt on the course spills over into the classroom activities."

"Most of the things you do as part of Dreams and Teams are things we should really be doing in the classroom everyday anyway."

"The system I use now in the classroom is totally different to what I did before."

"I've realised that the facilitation skills are crucial."

AND OF THEIR FEELINGS

"I've discovered that children are quite fearless. I've got to bite my tongue sometimes. Instead of throwing obstacles in their way, I've just got to trust them and believe in them."

"I was just watching the Young Leader organising the whole event. It was so nice just to be an overseer, just giving advice and support."

"I look at Dreams and Teams as part of nation building."

In the UK there are numerous similar projects. For example, following a successful pilot operated by Changemakers (http://www.changemakers.org.uk) and Education Extra (http://www.continyou.org.uk), a project has been rolled out nationwide. Schools which are involved offer students the opportunity to design and carry out projects following their own interests, with support from designated members of staff. Students have used this as an opportunity to follow their own interests and have produced a very wide range of projects, ranging from building a skate park to running fund-raising events, to introducing recycling schemes or building a sensory garden. What makes this approach different from traditional voluntary service is that students are encouraged and supported (as appropriate) to take control for themselves, to take risks, to work out for themselves what the problems may be, and to evaluate their own learning. Acknowledgement of their achievement is similar to that which takes place in the *Dreams and Teams* scheme in South Africa: a presentation event.

The *Health Promoting Schools* project (http://www.healthpromotingschools.co.uk) is being introduced through Active Citizens in Schools in one region of the UK. Schools are encouraged to form a group which includes young people as well as staff, to formulate their own *Health Promoting Schools* policy, looking at issues such as school environment, healthy eating and wider environmental issues such as sustainability and mental wellbeing. As with *Dreams and Teams* students are not just consulted, but are major players in designing their school's policy. Both are excellent examples of ways of engaging young people in the creation of their own society.

What is fascinating was that we, living in a mature democracy, are facing the same challenges and coming up with almost identical solutions to our colleagues in South Africa, a fledgling democracy.

Young people, participation and democracy

The disengagement of young people from the democratic process in the UK is well documented. An in-depth study of the levels of engagement of fourteen year olds found that:

> "An overwhelming four out of five students in all countries (including the UK) indicated that they do not intend to participate in the conventional political activities generally associated with adult political involvement: joining a party, writing letters to newspapers about social and political concerns, and being a candidate for a local or city office."
> (Torney-Purta *et al* 2001:12).

The maturity of the democracy seems to make little difference, nor does the previous regime: ex-socialist states seems to suffer from the same malaise as mature democracies:

> "Diverse patterns of civic knowledge and attitudes toward democratic participation are found in both newly-democratic countries and long-established democracies."
> (Torney-Purta *et al* 2001:16).

Teaching young people about democracy and political systems is clearly insufficient: if it was enough, then Civics, which many current educators endured in their formative years, would have led to large scale political involvement, this is clearly not the case.

However, young people are clearly not disengaged from politics, but from Politics – they are disengaged from our current party system, with all its flaws. Torney-Purta *et al* (2001) found that despite their apparent disinterest in formal politics (other than voting, which a high percentage of the international cohort saw as sufficient to fulfil their democratic responsibilities) fourteen year olds **were** prepared to take part in other forms of civic and political engagement.

Where young people are empowered to take control of projects, however minor, the impact is rapid and far-reaching. The problem in both countries that is preventing this happening appears to be attitudes *to* young people, rather than the attitudes *of* young people. In the UK the overwhelming media stereotype of young people is as troublemakers – we see very little of the positive input which young people make, hear very little of their successes. Too often young people are regarded as people who are not yet ready to be trusted. We are constantly bombarded with media hype about the 'yob culture' and not much less frequently with more and more punitive legislation designed to punish offenders.

As a society we have extended the period of childhood further and further until we accept that even those completing their degree in their early twenties are not really grown-ups. At this age, many of the previous generation were already parents with five years of working behind them. When they join the working world, their opinions count. In the UK the people we take seriously are the grown-ups (and working grown-ups at that). Osler and Starkey (2005), for example, argue that young people are perceived as citizens-in-waiting rather than as citizens in their own right.

In South Africa the problem appears to be different. It seems traditionally to be a more hierarchical society, with age being the criteria for movement up the scale. Young people have been regarded as less important than adults, and as such they expect, and are expected, to do the adults' bidding.

Both systems leave the young people disempowered, not because they are not capable of taking control, but because they are never given the opportunity. In the UK they are trusted to do very little; in South Africa they have traditionally been expected to do a great deal, but only what they are told to do. Osler and Starkey report one young person's opinion in England as:

> "They don't trust us to do anything properly. They treat us like babies and haven't even let us try. They don't want us to succeed, then they might have to treat us properly." (2005:51)

The paradox is that the very brightest minds, those people full of ideas and energy, are shackled in both countries. The majority are rarely given the opportunity to test their ideas out, rarely asked their opinion, prevented from taking risks; in short, they are frequently disempowered.

> "Young people often display a spiritual and material generosity towards others which can disappear by the time adulthood is reached. One of the challenges facing us is how to encourage children to retain that giving instinct and how to help them put it to best use." (Lord Chancellor's address to the Citizenship Foundation at the Law Society (27 January 1998) as quoted in Education for citizenship and the teaching of democracy in schools, Final report of the Advisory Group on Citizenship 22 September 1998.)

The failure to meet this particular challenge has resulted in a generation of young learners who are underachieving, not because they lack ability but because they lack opportunity: a generation who do not believe in their own abilities, because they have never had a chance to test them: a generation who lack goals, because they have not yet worked out where they want to go or who they want to be, *because they are not allowed to*.

The impact of allowing young people control over at least some aspect of their lives, of engaging them profitably in doing something for their community, and recognising that society is not something amorphous 'out there', but is actually the creation of all those who live in it, can be astounding. The impact of Active Citizenship on young people can be life changing. In my experience, truants turn into regular attenders, disruptive students turn into your favourite pupils, students with no focus find their niche. The impact is equally impressive on those who teach them: teachers can begin to see the real worth of students, appreciate them for what they can do rather than looking for what they can't do. The way teachers and pupils relate changes dramatically. (See also Davies, 1998, on the impact of school councils on pupil exclusion.)

If we want our young people to take leadership positions, we need to educate them early, to let them practise, to give them real responsibility. We need to let them take risks, fail, rewrite the script, and reflect on their learning. How else will they know how to operate as adults?

If there was ever any doubt about the ability of young people to lead the way, to really initiate change, it is the role of young people in the Soweto Uprising of 1976. It was dangerous and many children died, but that this was an event which shaped world history, and at its simplest level it was young people standing up for what they believed in, taking action, being citizens.

The need for a programme of education for democratic citizenship in South Africa may be self-evident: it is a relatively new democracy with a myriad of problems, not least of which is the still obvious legacy of apartheid. The people of South Africa are only too aware that something must be done. The UK may be more complacent, but the problem is no less pressing. Instead of vilifying young people, and thinking of ever new ways of punishing them, why not be proactive and prepare these young people to take an active role in shaping the society of the future?

KEY POINTS

- Democratic schools (and communities) require leadership at all levels and in all contexts.

- Innovative learning and teaching result in learning by all those involved – educator and learner.

- When learners take some responsibility for their own education it does not necessarily result in chaos – or make the educator redundant.

- Meaningful participation and control is likely to engender a response from relatively young learners.

- Future citizens of a meaningful democratic society require teachers who are democratic and schools that support democratic educators and learners.

SIGNPOSTS

- Clemitshaw, G. and Calvert, M. (2005) Implementing Citizenship in the English Secondary School Curriculum: A follow-up study. *Pastoral Care in Education*, 23 (3), pp31-036.

- Criddle, E., Vidovich, L. and O'Neill, M. (2004) Discovering democracy: an analysis of curriculum policy for citizenship education. *Westminster Studies in Education*, 27 (1), pp27-41.

- Ireland, E., Kerr, D., Lopes, J. and Nelson, J. with Cleaver, E. (2006) *Active Citizenship and Young People: Opportunities, Experiences and Challenges in and Beyond School*. London: DfES/NFER.

- Faulks, K. (2006) Education for citizenship in England's secondary schools: a critique of current principle and practice. *Journal of Education Policy*, 21 (1), pp59-74.

- Osler, A. and Starkey, H. (2003) Learning for Cosmopolitan Citizenship: theoretical debates and young people's experiences. *Educational Review*, 55 (3), pp243-253.

POINTS FOR DISCUSSION

- To what extent can schools be democratic?

- To what extent can teacher training institutions be democratic?

- How far are you democratic in your dealings with student teachers?

- What examples of democratic practice from the two case studies outlined above are reflected in your institution? … could you introduce to your colleagues?

CONCLUSION

Citizenship education is the right vehicle for such change.

> *We should not, must not, dare not, be complacent about the health and future of British democracy. Unless we become a nation of engaged citizens, our democracy is not secure ...*"
> (Education for citizenship and the teaching of democracy in schools, Final report of the Advisory Group on Citizenship 22 September 1998: 7,8)

It can be argued that schools that model democratic values, by promoting an open climate for discussing issues and inviting students to take part in shaping school life, are effective in promoting both civic knowledge and engagement. One major problem that was immediately evident to the group during the study visit to South Africa was that, on the whole, teaching at all levels has a tendency to be a didactic process. This applies to teacher training as much as to primary education. It was a 'revolution' for the teachers at Strelitzia to have been trained in *Dreams and Teams* methods and strategies. It had a profound impact on their relationships with students and on their classroom practice. This was partly because such approaches had previously not been part of the culture of education. It is understandable, in a young democracy, that some may not be aware of the need to develop the potential of future citizens to play an active part in the creation of their society. **The situation in the UK is, however, not all that different.**

The role of teacher education in creating the teachers of tomorrow and, therefore, shaping the future school climate, is crucial. The question which needs to be asked is how democratic are our teacher training institutions? How often do student teachers have the opportunity to play an active role in shaping their own experience?

There is significant evidence that active citizenship projects, such as *Dreams and Teams*, are required in both the UK and South Africa if the next generation of citizens are to be able to carry out the roles and responsibilities in democratic societies. For example, developing effective leaders cannot be left to chance and must be planned.

Future citizens need to be educated in democratic schools and in democratic classrooms and if education for democratic citizenship is to exist and be successful, it requires democratic teachers. In turn, **democratic teachers need to actually experience democratic and participatory methods when they are training.** Further, they must be consciously prepared to use such methods in schools and classrooms. Currently, this is a substantial challenge for teacher education.

REFERENCES

Davies, L. (1998) *School Councils and Pupil Exclusion*. London: School Councils UK.

Osler, A. and Starkey, H. (2005) *Changing Citizenship: Democracy and Inclusion in Education*. Maidenhead: Open University Press.

Torney-Purta, J., Lehmann, R., Oswald, H. and Schulz, W. (2001) *Citizenship and Education in Twenty-eight Countries: Civic Knowledge and Engagement at Age Fourteen*. Amsterdam: International Association for the Evaluation of Educational Achievement.

CHAPTER 9:
SCHOOLS AND SUSTAINABILITY

DOREEN OAKLEY, UNIVERSITY OF LEEDS

"Humankind has not woven the web of life; we are but one thread within it. Whatever we do to the web, we do to ourselves. All things are bound together. All things connect."
Chief Seattle 1786-1866

INTRODUCTION

This holistic view of the world, that individuals do not act in isolation and that humanity and nature cannot be separated is at the heart of the Green Agenda. The quest for economic growth may have led many societies to ignore the social and political dimensions of 'development', with consequent claims from green activists that it has brought increasing damage to the environment and social fabric on which our well-being depends. There is a growing agenda of concern relating to : energy supply; the debate about nuclear power; global warming; climate change; pollution; waste etc. **How can teachers help pupils make sense of these complicated issues? What role do teacher educators have in enabling future teachers?**

AGENDA 21

The UN Report Agenda 21 (1992:1) stated,

"Humanity stands at a defining moment in history. We are confronted with a perpetuation of disparities between and within nations, a worsening of poverty, hunger, ill health and illiteracy, and the continuing deterioration of the ecosystems on which we depend for our well-being. However, integration of environment and development concerns and greater attention to them will lead to the fulfilment of basic needs, improved living standards for all, better protected and managed ecosystems and a safer, more prosperous future. No nation can achieve this on its own; but together we can - in a global partnership for sustainable development."

Agenda 21 is a comprehensive plan of action to be taken nationally and locally by organizations in every area in which humanity impacts on the environment.

Agenda 21 posits that population, consumption and technology are the primary driving forces of environmental change and lays out what needs to be done to reduce wasteful and inefficient consumption patterns in some parts of the world while encouraging increased but sustainable development in others.

Agenda 21 generated a range of policies and programmes designed to achieve a sustainable balance between consumption, population and the Earth's life-supporting capacity. It describes some of technologies and techniques that need to be developed to provide for human needs while carefully managing natural resources.

Agenda 21 provides options for combating degradation of the land, air and water, conserving forests and the diversity of species of life. It deals with poverty and excessive consumption, health and education, cities and farmers. Within it can be identified roles for everyone: governments, business people, trade unions, scientists, *teachers*, and, not least, ordinary people in their daily lives.

Agenda 21 sees sustainable development as the way to reverse both poverty and environmental destruction.

Agenda 21 states that the measure of a wealth of a country needs to count the cost of the full value of natural resources and the full cost of environmental degradation. The polluter should, in principle, bear the costs of pollution. To reduce the risk of causing damage, environmental assessment should be carried out before starting projects that carry the risk of adverse impacts. Governments should reduce or eliminate subsidies that are not consistent with sustainable development.

Agenda 21 also highlights the need to eradicate poverty by giving poor people more access to the resources they need to live sustainably.

Agenda 21 proposes that industrialized countries have a greater role in cleaning up the environment than poor nations, and a role in funding to help other nations develop in ways that have lower environmental impacts.

Agenda 21 calls on governments to adopt national strategies for sustainable development. These should be developed with wide participation, including non-government organizations and the public.

Agenda 21 puts most of the responsibility for leading change on national governments, but says they need to work in a broad series of partnerships with international organizations, business, regional, state, provincial and local governments, non-governmental and citizens' groups.

Agenda 21 explicitly made the link between environmental issues and social justice as well as emphasising the need for grass roots level participation.

Having accepted Agenda 21, the UK government has recently stated that the goals of sustainable development will be pursued through a sustainable, innovative and productive economy that delivers high levels of employment, that is a just society promoting social inclusion, sustainable communities and personal well being and has committed to a 60% reduction in greenhouse gas emissions by 2050 (Securing the Future, 2004). Environmental education has evolved into Education for Sustainable Development (ESD) and it seems to be widely accepted that the concept should be taught in schools with ESD being defined as:

> "enabling people to develop the knowledge, values and skills to participate in decisions about the way we do things, individually and collectively, both locally and globally that will improve the quality of life without damaging the planet in the future." (Huckle, 2004:33)

SCHOOLS AND SUSTAINABILITY IN ENGLAND AND SOUTH AFRICA

England and South Africa afford us the opportunity to compare how the issue of sustainability is being addressed both within the school curriculum and within more general practices in schools in two countries exhibiting different features of economic growth.

In England a number of National Curriculum subjects promote ESD through their cross curricular themes e.g. in Geography, under 'promoting spiritual, social and cultural development',

"… helping pupils to consider the impact of their own and other's actions, such as dropping litter or to investigate environmental issues, such as global warming, in which people's current needs have to be balanced against the needs of future generations'. Under the heading 'Promoting citizenship' the Geography document states that teachers should be, 'developing pupils' understanding of the world as a global community and the issues and challenges of global interdependence and responsibility." (8)

Most importantly the document states that, *"Geography plays a significant part in promoting education for sustainable development through:*

- *developing pupils' knowledge and understanding of the concept of sustainable development and the skills to act upon this*

- *developing pupils' knowledge and understanding of key concepts of sustainable development, such as interdependence, quality of life and diversity*

- *developing pupils' skills of critical enquiry and an ability to handle and interpret information*

- *exploring values and attitudes about complex issues, such as resource use and development."* (9)

The Geography Programmes of Study include ESD at each Key Stage as follows;

"Pupils should be taught to:

- *recognise changes to the environment and recognise how the environment may be improved and sustained. (KS1)*

- *recognise how people can improve the environment or damage it, and how decisions about places and environments affect the future quality of people's lives and recognise how and why people may seek to manage environments sustainably, and to identify opportunities for their own involvement. (KS2)*

- *describe and explain environmental change and recognise different ways of managing it and explore the idea of sustainable development and recognise its implications for people, places and environments and for their own lives. (KS3)"* (17)

Specific reference is also made to ESD within the Citizenship National Curriculum at Key Stage 4 i.e. *"the wider issues and challenges of global interdependence and responsibility, including sustainable development and Local Agenda 21."* (19) In addition, ESD features in the non-statutory guidelines for PSHE (QCA, 2000:23). It might be argued that ESD does not have a natural home within the overall National Curriculum and so could easily 'get lost' but one may speculate that Geography is where ESD is most commonly taught.

In South Africa since the 1994 election, the South African Department for Education has recognised the contribution of ESD as being vital in terms of valuing and conserving the environment as well as moving towards social justice.

Underpinning the new South African Curriculum for 2005 is a set of ten values which seeks to promote through a series of educational strategies the ideal that South Africans will be able to live decently now and in the future (Carter, Harber and Serf, 2003: Ch.3). Geography is not a distinct subject in its own right under the new curriculum but is part of the Social Sciences. As in England, ESD seems to have 'found a home' within the Geography element of this part of the curriculum, where *"human rights; critical awareness of environmental and social issues; how people respond to and influence the environment; understanding of how social and environmental justice can be brought about through actions of individuals and organisations; the making of critical and informed choices and taking action to deal with social and environmental issues"* are all listed as components. (Carter, *et al,* 2003:60).

Within the South African outcomes-based curriculum the Revised National Curriculum Statement (RNCS:6) of 2002 states that *"In Geography, learners will explore:*

- *social inequality and forms of exploitation with regard to environmental and land issues;*
- *the decreasing availability of resources;*
- *the deteriorating quality of the environment; and*
- *strategies for change."*

All three learning outcomes for Geography could be viewed as promoting the ESD agenda:

- Learning Outcome 1: The learner will be able to use enquiry skills to investigate geographical and environmental concepts and processes.
- Learning Outcome 2: The learner will be able to demonstrate geographical and environmental knowledge and understanding.
- Learning Outcome 3: The learner will be able to make informed decisions about social and environmental issues and problems.

As in the English curriculum, knowledge for each stage of the learners development is suggested e.g. for Learning Outcome 3 at Grade 2 *"actions that could be taken to improve places in the local environment"* is stated while at Grade 9 *"principles of Agenda 21, such as the need for everybody to participate in the management of resources"* and *"the need for all our actions to ensure future sustainability"* and *"the need for everybody to be actively involved in addressing environmental problems"* are all stated.

How successful teaching ESD and other concepts might be within the Geography framework *"would depend largely on the depth of the teacher's knowledge and expertise of teaching Geography"* (Le Grange and Beets, 2005:269). Although referring specifically to the South African curriculum, this statement surely holds true for England too. Further, Le Grange and Beets mention the danger that teachers *"schooled in a textbook based behaviourist approach to Geography education might find security in the content defined in RCNS"*. This fear of being creative within a relatively open curriculum may be something that English teachers fear too.

ESD IN PRACTICE

A huge challenge facing schools and teachers everywhere is summarised in Kofi Annan's words, *"Our biggest challenge in this century is to take an idea that sounds abstract – sustainable development – and turn it into reality for all the world's people."* (2001:2)

DFID (2005:19) argues that,

> *"What is taught in the classroom is reinforced if children and young people see this as reflected in the practice of the school. Schools can practise sustainable development by using fair trade products and ethical banking, practising 'rethink, reuse, repair, recycle' and having a green purchasing policy. The development of ethical practice can involve children and young people, for example, through a school council. Children and young people need to be supported to make links between the school's ethical practice and the global dimension."*

This raises an important question: should schools of the future be living and working examples of sustainable development?

Ofsted (2003:6) identified some examples of sustainable schools whilst admitting that these remain few in number. Motives for establishing sustainable schools may include reduced costs, improved staff morale, stronger relationships with the local community and perhaps even better behaved pupils.

In looking at examples of sustainable practice within schools at present, one can identify a continuum reaching from a 'tinkering at the edges' approach, e.g. some recycling of soft drink cans, through the 'eco-school' approach to the 'full blown green school'. Not surprisingly one can find many examples of the first, fewer of the second and very few of the third in both England and South Africa alike.

Below are just a few examples of the first approach in action in both countries. In England, in Ovenden, near Halifax, Moorside Junior School during the summer of 2005 created a 'Culture Club' garden where they grew fresh vegetables and herbs in raised beds for sale alongside home-made cakes and biscuits. Land is being cleared for a similar scheme at Strelizia School in Durban, South Africa.

In England, at Riverside Junior School, Hebden Bridge, the catering manager sources local food and has opened a breakfast club for pupils who might otherwise not have a meal before school starts. In South Africa, Durban Girls' High School operates a similar scheme to provide children from the more deprived areas of Durban with food before school begins. Also in Hebden Bridge, at Calder High School, an interactive renewable energy garden has been created to support the Science curriculum at KS3 and 4. Examples of recycling e.g. of paper or printer cartridges are relatively widespread in both countries.

Perhaps a difference between the two countries can be seen in the way that green issues might be linked with 'pride in being a citizen of the new South Africa' as exemplified in the litter bin at Strelizia School painted with the South African flag. Compare this colourful article to the ones normally seen around English schools.

Compostable toilets (at Ndabirhono Primary School) and a water supply collected in a butt (at Magoda Primary) could be seen as extreme examples of sustainability in practice in English school. Yet these two examples are a necessity in the relatively deprived schools in the area of

Richmond to the west of Durban. Is it the case that in England is sustainability in schools a 'nicety' whereas in at least some schools in South Africa it is a necessity?

The middle or eco school approach represents a more whole school, multi-faceted approach to sustainability. Model policies for eco schools i.e. working with existing built schools, are increasingly common in England and widely available on the Internet as are audits with which one can assess the 'greenness' of a school. *"Successful learning occurs best where there is a comprehensive, whole school approach … which reinforces the sustainable message."* (Ofsted, 2003:9) This report gives details of a primary school where the Head began by having a private consultant consider the school's energy consumption, followed up by a display of the findings and the development of an action plan. Each classroom now has notes about energy saving and has two eco-monitors whose role it is to make checks. The report further points out that this approach is frequently better organised in primary schools than secondary schools. Is this because such schemes are easier to organise in a smaller scale environment? Is it that younger pupils are more willing to be active participants? A further point made by the report is the missed opportunity to link practice with theory i.e. in relatively few schools is the opportunity to raise awareness about and for pupils to learn about 'wastefulness' taken up and linked with recycling practice.

The Eco-Schools Programme provides English schools with a framework to enable a school to analyse its operations and become more sustainable. It claims that by following the programme a school *"will become a more stimulating place in which to learn, whilst reducing the environmental impact of the whole school on the community."* (Eco-Schools) Amongst a number of claims made are: pupils will *"take responsibility for the environmental management and they will develop an increased sense of responsibility for their surroundings."* On the back of this increased sense of belonging and pride according to the programme comes *"a reported improvement in the behaviour of pupils."* With current concerns about pupils' behaviour in schools in England being in the limelight, this must be a notable point.

The concept of global footprints is used in many primary and secondary schools to raise awareness. An interesting idea is one where pupils accessed a French-Canadian website using both their language and their ICT skills in order to consider and then write about the issue in French. As the report concludes *"… such schools can provide inspiration for other schools to take the first steps towards a fully integrated model for ESD that permeates the whole curriculum."*

Finally, the 'full blown' green school is perhaps the ultimate dream for supporters of ESD. This invariably means a 'new build'. Until recently this might have been seen as a pipedream in both countries and still might be in South Africa. However, the recently announced *Building Schools for the Future* (BSF) initiative, with its funding for new buildings, may bring at least some dreams nearer to reality within the next few years. For example, capital investment in school buildings will be £2.2 billion during 2005-2006. Meanwhile a few examples of 'green schools' do exist already. One of these is Kingsmead Primary School in Northwich which was opened in September 2004 as part of the BSF initiative at a cost of £2.4 million. This is described as *"an 'ultra-modern, eco-friendly"* school. It is mainly constructed of timber and *"is so intelligent that it can open and close its own windows to suit weather conditions."* (Teachers' Magazine 2004, Issue 35:1) The boiler uses recycled woodchips for fuel, and rainwater is collected in a trough on the roof for using to flush toilets. Solar panels are used to power the building. Further, this school combines the practice with theory by including two outdoor classrooms: a butterfly garden and a vegetable patch. Weather monitors and transparent rainwater pipes allow children to apply knowledge about ESD in a real context. Within the secondary sector, Lauder College in Dunfermline, Scotland is perhaps an example of future developments. It is due to open in August 2006 at a cost of £4.5 million and promises to be *"a sustainable workshop for the 21st Century"* (SD Commission).

TEACHER EDUCATION

Huckle (2005:45) writes, *"the education of teachers should take place in institutions that are striving to be models of sustainable development."* If newly qualified teachers are to become advocates for the idea that there should be a greater alignment between rhetoric and reality within schools, then perhaps it would be helpful if they encountered sustainability in practice within their HE institution. Some institutions are highly committed with sustainability high on the management's agenda and visible to all whilst others have barely 'begun to walk'.

At one end of the continuum are institutions such as Harvard whose commitment extends to employing a Director for Sustainable Development with 13 full time staff with a mission to make *"America's oldest institute of higher education a model of environmental sustainability, offering a world of hope to this year's graduates and those of years to come."* (Harvard Green Campus Initiative) The strategy of having a dedicated team is that action is taken on the rhetoric *between* meetings and progress is therefore made more rapidly. Projects range in scale. Large-scale projects include new buildings and refits with sustainability at the forefront, providing subsidised public transport, eliminating the use of toxic chemicals and using 100% recycled paper products in the cleaning regime. Smaller scale projects including recycling are often the result of encouraging behavioural changes amongst groups of colleagues within one building. Successful peer to peer training and best practice exchanges between departments seems to engender change effectively.

It may be that universities are making changes that might not always be obvious to students. To address this, Harvard makes explicit its actions on its website and in student newspapers, and by attempting to include students by having them sign an online pledge to become more sustainable citizens. Harvard's Director of Sustainability summarises her belief about the important role that HE has: *"If universities do not address sustainability, they will not look smart"*. (Sharp, 2005)

In the UK a number of HE institutions such as The University of Gloucester and Leeds Metropolitan University have made steps in the 'journey towards sustainability'. At Gloucester, the new sports science facility included using sustainable practices within its construction e.g. crushing demolished buildings material to use as foundations for the new build and having solar panels on the roof to provide 17% of the building's energy needs. At one of its other campuses a new centre for teaching and learning is being constructed which will use 40% recycled materials, with the 'on site waste' problem being reduced by the use of pre-fabrication of units. These large projects can be put alongside the more modest, but arguably more visible to the students, projects such as using 100% recycled paper for photocopiers and printers, PCs fitted with power saving devices, offering free public transport to students within the Gloucestershire area, using electric vehicles on campus and sourcing fair trade and/or local food. Gloucester's commitment is being made explicit to its students through a column on sustainability issues in the students' fortnightly newspaper.

An HE institution is a business with the subsequent need to reduce its costs. Sustainable practices such as recycling and reducing energy use clearly have a role to play in this. However, there is a school of thought that suggests that student recruitment and retention is linked to an institution's commitment to sustainability. (CABE, 2005) This may depend on many factors, not least being whether the sustainability is visible to the students and may be disputed under the present regulations. However, with new regulations imminent, the cost of not moving towards sustainability may become an issue for financial planners within institutions. To this end, *"Will universities pull or be pushed into to adaptation and mitigation of climate change?"* (Nicholson, 2005)

At institutions such as the University of Leeds there are many medium and small-scale initiatives taking place. These include projects such as recycling office waste, increasing the number of cycle racks on campus, providing 'pay as you go' car hire by the hour and providing a monthly payment plan to buy yearly bus passes. Energy audits on buildings are being carried out and a carbon dioxide reduction target has been set. Some electricity is purchased from renewable sources. Water consumption has been reduced by 23% over the last 5 years. It is recommended to departments that recycled paper is purchased and that any new printers bought have a double-sided facility. Green waste is shredded and composted, garden chemical use and the use of peat based products are the subject of yearly reduction targets and more 'wildlife friendly' shrubs, trees and herbaceous perennials are being planted. 'Fairtrade' status has been applied for and in the near future it is hoped that Leeds will offer cycle loans as a tax-free benefit.

Can we ever achieve the 'whole institution approach' whereby ESD leads to sustainable practice which leads to sustainable institutions being an educational tool because they offer a model of good practice? A HEFCE Report (2005) states that there is a high level of consensus within HE on the importance of sustainable development but that there is little consensus as to the way forward. Further, it recognised the potential contribution that this sector has within its role as educators through the generation and transfer of knowledge, leadership of and influence on, local, national and international networks.

TEACHER EDUCATION

How green is present teacher education? With the exception of pockets of good practice e.g. Bangor (Bennell, 2005), probably not very. This is worrying when one considers the complexities of teaching sustainability. The Geographical Association (GA) describes ESD as technically challenging teaching which requires teachers to engage pupils in a culture of argument, complexity, uncertainty and risk analysis. The GA further adds that they have concerns that ITT and CPD are not equipping teachers with the skills and knowledge necessary to teach ESD in the cross-curricular manner that the QCA advocates (GA, 2003). The UN recognised the need to pay special attention to the training of teachers in a report in 1997, so much so that it has gone on to designate 2005-2015 as *The Decade of Education for Sustainable Development*.

Webster (2001) outlines in detail what teachers need. These include the following:

- a considerable amount of knowledge and understanding from natural and social sciences, the arts and humanities i.e. ESD needs to be cross-curricular;

- the ability to recognise the contribution of their particular subject towards giving some understanding of environmental education (Palmer, 1998) and to development education (Osler, 1994);

- a recognition that subject knowledge could be more inclusive of ideas about alternative technology;

- a recognition that citizenship education offers an opportunity to explore alternative forms of citizenship and democracy so giving alternative views of the environment and of development;

- the ability to audit lessons using key questions such as: Is this a real issue? Are my lessons future orientated? Do my lessons feature viable alternatives?

Huckle (2005) outlines what student teachers need as follows:

- to recognise that we are both part of nature, yet apart from nature i.e. we are part of a biological species, dependent on ecological resources yet partly independent because our powers of language and technology use enable us to transform our own nature and that which surrounds us;

- to be encouraged to be 'weak anthropocentrics' because in so being we can best promote mutual flourishing of human and non-human nature because holding a 'strong ecocentric' view might 'romanticise' nature whilst holding 'strongly anthropocentric/technocratic' views might favour exploitation and oppression of nature;
- to recognise that democratic values such as freedom, equality, justice and respect for human rights are important because in a truly democratic society people are more likely to be able to recognise and realise a common interest.

There are different approaches to how ESD might be included within the ITE curriculum. It may be that a School of Education might believe sufficiently in ESD that they would include it in such a way that it permeates all teaching and other activities. It could be offered as a separate discipline. It could be offered as part of a course as a module.

The *Learning to Last Initiative* (2002-03) stressed the importance of the TTA working with the National College of School Leadership and teacher training institutions to develop a strategic approach to teacher training for ESD alongside the current initiative to train teachers in citizenship education, drawing upon lessons learned in other areas of the curriculum such as IT where teachers have had to learn new skills quickly.

KEY POINTS

- The need for sustainability has never been more pressing. Therefore, the time to promote ESD in schools has never been more right.

- Both South Africa and the UK have chosen to include ESD in their National Curricula and both countries now face the immediate problem of developing teachers' knowledge so that it does not remain 'a paper exercise'.

- Schools and teachers face the choice of being passive providers or active participators within the ESD process.

- Models of good practice already exist within South Africa and the UK.

SIGNPOSTS

- www.heepi.org.uk/green_gown_award_winners.htm

- http://www.esdgc-wales.org.uk/english/Teacher_Education/default.htm

- http://www.qca.org.uk/282_858.html

- http://www.qca.org.uk/2812.html

- Butt, G. (2003) Establishing principles for the creation of a Geography and Citizenship course in Initial Teacher Education (ITE), in (2004) *Papers from Geography and Citizenship Education: Research Perspectives: Conference held at the University of London Institute of Education April 2003*, edited by Kent, A. and Powell, A. London: International Geographical Union Commission of Geographical Education British Sub-Committee, pp21-31.

- Shallcross, T. *et al* (2006) 'Promoting sustainable development through whole school approaches: an international, intercultural teacher education research and development project'. *Journal of Education for Teaching* 32,3 pp283-301.

- Stolman, J. and Dechano, L. (2002) Political Geography, Geographical Education and Citizenship. *Geojournal Library*, 71, pp127-144.

- Tilbury, D. (2002) Active Citizenship: Empowering People as Cultural Agents Through Geography in Gerber, R. and Williams, M. (2002) *Geography, Culture and Education*. Netherlands: Kluwer Academic Publishers, pp105-113.

POINTS FOR DISCUSSION

- Do I see ESD as an essential part of the institution in which I work and of the curriculum, embedded within it, rather than a 'bolt on'?

- How sustainable is your own present lifestyle and what changes could you make?

- What changes would you like to see in your institution and how could you contribute towards these?

CONCLUSION

Learning to live more sustainably can be seen as a major challenge for all countries but especially for industrialised ones. Alternatively, we can view it as an opportunity, because it should offer the Earth's population a less damaging, healthier and, perhaps, more fulfilling lifestyle, a higher degree of social justice, a more secure world that puts us into balance with each other and with the physical world, that recognises our existence as 'a thread within the web'. To achieve this I believe that education may need to shift radically to include new forms of knowledge and new ways of organising knowledge.

ESD should not be a 'bolt on' but be part of a shift in culture, thinking and educational practice. New ways of teaching and learning such as a more skills based pedagogy to promote thinking skills and enquiry learning will be needed. I believe some teachers, especially Geography teachers are already moving towards this approach. However, the question remains, through ITT, ITE and CPD, are we thoroughly preparing teachers for the challenges involved?

REFERENCES

The United Nations Department of Economic and Social Affairs (1992) *Agenda 21. Report of the United Nations Conference on Environment and Development* (Rio de Janeiro, 3-14 June 1992) posted online at http://www.un.org/documents/ga/conf151/aconf15126-1annex1.htm The United Nations Department of Economic and Social Affairs (DESA).

Annan, K. UN Press Release: SC/SM/7739 15/03/01.

Bennell, S. J. (2005) *Educating for Global Citizenship* downloadable from http://www.bangor.ac.uk/

CABE (Commission for Architecture and the Built Environment) (2005) *Design with Distinction: The Value of Good Building Design in Higher Education*. London: CABE.

Department of Education (2001) Manifesto on Values, Education and Democracy, *in* Carter, C., Harber, C. and Serf, J. (2003) *Towards Ubuntu*. Birmingham: Development Education Centre.

Department of Education (2002) *Revised National Curriculum Statement Grades R-9 (Schools) Policy*. Pretoria: Department of Education.

DfEE/QCA (1999) *National Curriculum for England: Geography*. London: Department for Education and Employment and Qualifications and Curriculum Authority.

DfES (2004) Bright Green *in Teachers' Magazine* (November 2004). London: Teachernet/DfES - downloadable at www.teachernet.gov.uk

DFID (2005) *Developing the global dimension in the school curriculum*. London: Department for International Development, Department for Education and Skills and Qualifications and Curriculum Authority.

Eco-Schools programme at www.eco-schools.org.uk

Geographical Association (2003) *Learning the Sustainability Lesson. Environmental Audit Committee Report*. Sheffield: The Geographical Association, paragraph 86.

Green, D. quoted in Job, D. (1996) Geography and environmental education – an exploration of perspectives and strategies, *in* Kent, A., Lambert, D., Naish, M. and Slater, F. *Geography in Education – Viewpoints on Teaching and Learning*. Cambridge: Cambridge University Press.

Harvard Green Campus Initiative. See details at www.greencampus.harvard.edu

Higher Education Funding Council for England (2005) *Sustainable Development in Higher Education: Statement of Policy*. London: HEFC.

Huckle, J. (2004) *Education for Sustainable Development: A briefing paper for the TTA.* London: TTA.

Learning to Last Initiative (2002-03) Learning and Skills Development Agency downloadable at http://www.lsda.org.uk/Sustainable/Toolkit

Le Grange, L. and Beets, P. (2005) Geography Education in South Africa after a Decade of Democracy. *Geography,* 90 (3), pp267-277.

Nicholson, Robin (commissioner at CABE). Quotation from his speech at the conference 'Creating Tomorrow's Campus'. Leeds 1/12/05.

Ofsted (2003) *Taking the first step forward … towards education for sustainable development. Good practice in primary and secondary schools.* London: Ofsted.

Osler A. (1994) *in* Huckle, J. (2004) *Education for Sustainable Development: A briefing paper for the TTA.* London: TTA.

Palmer (1998) *in* Huckle, J. (2004) *Education for Sustainable Development: A briefing paper for the TTA.* London: TTA.

SD Commission Sustainable Development Commission *Sustainable Places* downloadable at http://sd-commission.org.uk

Sharp, L. (Director of Sustainable Development, Harvard University) Quotation from her speech at the conference 'Creating Tomorrow's Campus'. University of Leeds 01/12/05.

SUSchool's Newsletter (Spring 2005), downloadable at www.suschool.org.uk

UK Government (2004) *Securing the Future.* London: HMSO.

Webster (2001) *in* Huckle, J. (2004) *Education for Sustainable Development: A briefing paper for the TTA.* London: TTA.

CHAPTER 10:
THE CHALLENGES OF TEACHING MUSIC IN A GLOBAL CITIZENSHIP CONTEXT

JENNY HUGHES, UNIVERSITY COLLEGE, WORCESTER

INTRODUCTION

Training Teachers for tomorrow; the Vision statement for Global Citizenship from the Development Education Association (1998) argues that students and teachers can become active global citizens working towards a more sustainable and equitable future through:

"acknowledging their own role in society and their interrelationship with the local, national, and global environments;

recognising the dignity and worth of every human being;

celebrating what we all have in common with our fellow human beings, in our rich diversity of cultures and traditions."

The citizenship curriculum in England (DfEE/QCA, 1999) includes references to consideration of how pupils and teachers relate to the wider world both nationally and globally; for example, at Key Stage Three, pupils should be taught about *"the world as a global community, and the political, economic, environmental and social implications of this …"* (para. 1i of *Knowledge and Understanding about becoming informed citizens*). Government reports such as *Every Child Matters*, and *All Our Futures, Creativity, Culture, and Education*, include specific reference to the potential role of arts subjects, including music, in general citizenship education. Guidelines concerned specifically with the teaching of global citizenship, from a range of respected non-governmental organisations, for example OXFAM, also include similar statements. *"We see a Global Citizen as someone who … has an understanding of how the world works economically, politically, socially, **culturally**, technologically, and environmentally …"* (OXFAM website)

Music is often overlooked, by both teacher educators and by those responsible for leading the teaching of citizenship in schools, as a subject which might contribute to learning in what are considered more 'serious' or 'controversial' curriculum areas. And yet, the varied and stimulating material quoted in the previous paragraph does make reference to the important role of culture and the arts in developing pupils' understanding of their place in the world. For music educators two related themes would seem to emerge; firstly, that of celebrating and valuing musically what we have in common with our fellow human beings and secondly, of developing understanding of difference through active engagement with music from a range of traditions and cultures.

The first theme might also be expressed as thinking of the arts as a means of understanding ourselves and our interrelationships with others:

"The arts are concerned with understanding, and expressing, the qualities of human experiences. Through music, dance, visual arts, drama, and the rest, we try to give form to the feelings and perceptions that move us most as human beings: our experiences of love, grief, and belonging, and isolation, and all the currents of feeling that constitute our experience of self and others. It is through the arts in all forms that young people experiment with and try to articulate their deepest feelings and their own sense of cultural identity and belonging." (DfEE, 1999:69)

The recent publication of *Every Child Matters*, which will form the basis of educational policy and practice in England, includes an example of community cooperation in Birmingham, involving the Royal Ballet working with pupils, parents, and teachers, and using the different cultural backgrounds and experiences of the participants (DfES, 2004:15).

The second theme, that of engagement with the arts as a means of celebrating cultural diversity, is also discussed in *All Our Futures*:

"A balanced arts education has essential roles in the creative and cultural development of young people. First, the arts are essential to intellectual development … intelligence is multifaceted. The arts illustrate this diversity and provide practical ways of promoting it in all children … the arts are the most vivid expressions of human culture. To understand other cultures and ways of seeing, we need to engage with their music, visual art, verbal and performing arts where in many ways the pulse of culture beats most strongly."
(DfEE, 1999:69-70)

So let's get on with it

In recent years, music educators in England, supported by the National Curriculum programmes of study, have established the principle that the essential elements of music education are practical engagement in composition, performance, listening and appraisal. Teachers have been given relative freedom, compared with other National Curriculum subjects, to decide upon actual curriculum content. The National Curriculum merely specifies that musical knowledge, skills, and understanding be taught through a range of live and recorded music from different times and cultures, including music from the British Isles, the Western classical tradition, folk, jazz, and popular genres, and by well-known composers and performers. It is generally agreed in England that some practical engagement with music of non-Western cultures is beneficial for pupils' musical development. Stock (2002:182) argues persuasively;

"Musical concepts and habits that we have acquired through the enculturation process, through being born and bred within a particular culture, are sometimes overlooked; they become so 'natural' that we may no longer be able to perceive them. Studying a different musical culture brings these issues back to our attention, and thereby encourages a deeper understanding of our own music."

Musicians the world over have always been curious about each other's practice, and the result has been many examples of works which arise out of cross-fertilisation between musical cultures. Debussy's fascination with the sonorities of the Javanese gamelan he heard at the World Exhibition in Paris in 1889 and subsequent inclusion of antique cymbals in *L'aprés-midi d'une faune* in 1894 is a good example from the Western classical tradition. The current popularity in England of Bhangra, which can take the form of a vocal style and use of instruments found in many Indian musics, combined with rhythms and chord progressions found in western popular music, also comes to mind. South Africa is particularly rich in cross-fertilisations; the inclusion in indigenous musics of chord progressions from nineteenth century hymns taught by European missionaries being an example. In every case, the result of the encounter with musics from more than one culture has been fruitful and has expanded the language of music itself. Fortunately there have been for many years in the UK some excellent advocates for the teaching of music from different cultures; Robert Mawuena Kwami is a notable example. His writings have been a sustained attempt to enable music teachers in the UK to engage with, understand, and teach something of the principles and practices of black African cultures. Gerry Farrell advocated study of not only classical and popular Indian music in India itself, but also of Indian popular music in the West, such as Bhangra, and produced resources to support the teaching of this music in school.

Those attempting to introduce a wider musical and cultural perspective into music teaching do run the risk of being accused of tokenism. It is indeed true that music teachers in the UK cannot reproduce the atmosphere, circumstances, instruments, and even vocal techniques of musical practices in distant countries. Robert Mawuena Kwami, however, argues that teachers need to adopt a 'broad cultural perspective' which is 'inclusive and global', and to avoid an approach which is primarily a study based upon Western musics. He advocates sensitivity, reminding us that the classroom as the context for musical performance may *"ensure the application of equal opportunities in relation to such issues as gender, race, religion, and so on. For example, girls should play instruments that they would not be allowed to play in a traditional context."* (Kwami, 2001:151) He suggests that musics which are too closely linked to particular religious, social, and cultural conventions may need to be excluded. He stresses the importance of all participants being aware of the context of the music being performed; for example, in the majority of musical cultures around the world, the music played is not written down. The whole notion of musical structure can vary: *"In examining African music with 'Western spectacles', the architectural design of, say, a West African drum ensemble music could be explained in terms of polyrhythm or polymeter … such a perspective loses the holistic view – that everything is linked in the ensemble, there really is not conflict between the parts, they complement one another."* (Kwami, 2001:149) Despite all these caveats, however, he still argues that the arguments in favour of an 'inclusive and global' approach outweigh the obstacles.

ANY OBJECTIONS?

Debates around the question of multiculturalism/interculturalism in terms of what these words mean and whether they are merely the northern European imposing their view of culture on everyone regardless, yet again, have continued for many decades. The very act of, for example, learning about instruments from around the world, categorising them, comparing etc., could be regarded as a Western methodology – so therefore are we straying into controversial territory if we engage in such apparently harmless activity? It could equally be argued, however, that not to be open to different musical cultures and to try and understand them, actually sets up a dangerous situation of potential segregation, leading to ignorance and bigotry. In a recent, informative and well-researched article, for example, Bunting (2005:13-15) writes of the importance for teachers to be aware of and understanding the multi-faceted relationships which exist between music and followers of different traditions in Islam in England today. He argues for a dialogue with parents and community leaders and advocates that teachers become familiar with the vast repertoire of Islamic music, and with the values from which it springs.

Different musical cultures in South Africa

The current diversity of approaches to the study of a range of musical cultures in England can be traced back to the gradual development of a philosophy of music education, having its origins in initiatives of the early 1970s largely inspired by inspirational figures such as John Paynter. The challenges facing South African music educators today arise from a much less gradual process of evolution. They exist because of the very recent past in that country. During the apartheid regime, indigenous African music in particular in South Africa was not valued, often even by many from the communities making such music. Collected and recorded by and only available to a few scholars, this music was thought to be culturally inferior by the vast majority of the dominant white minority of the apartheid regime. Today, a musical resurrection and wider dissemination of these indigenous musics is currently taking place. A very popular and easily accessible collection of the traditional music of South Africa, which consists of an illustrated book and accompanying CD contains a quote which sums up the situation:

> "The Drumcafe's Traditional Music of South Africa is a true musical journey to the many different styles of indigenous music we had in the past, still and will always have, in and around South Africa. Dating back to many, many generations, it addresses very important issues about who we are; where we come from and where we go from here. And in its own humble way also offers us a true way of really seeing ourselves as an African nation in every sense of the word and allows us to be proud to be South Africans." (Levine, 2005)

So the immediate challenge for music educators in South Africa is to broaden the curriculum subject content and reflect a truly inclusive approach, making use of musics from the many different musical cultures, including African (Zulu, Xhosa, Venda, Bapedi, for example), Indian, Cape Coloured, Afrikaaner, Scottish, English, French, and others, which exist within South Africa itself. The revised National Curriculum Statement for Arts and Culture is explicit on this point:

> "To deal with the legacy of cultural intolerance and to prepare youth for the future, learners need to experience, understand and affirm the diversity of South African cultures. The effect of past imbalances is that there has been a strong influence by international cultures, and weak development and support of local arts and culture. Learners need to recognise the value of their own culture. This learning area addresses these imbalances."
> (www.polity.org.za/html/govdocs/policy/2002)

So what's similar to England?

This call to recognise and value arts and culture, including music, from the whole range of cultures which exist within South Africa has been eagerly responded to by music educators. During the early years of the new South Africa, music educators began to redress the former imbalances with collections of songs and musical activities drawn from a wider range of sources. The Centre for Music Education at the University of Pretoria, for example, published such collections (see details at the end of this chapter), and postgraduate music educators from all over Africa are currently studying there and making a great contribution to developing a culturally diverse music curriculum. One student, for example, regularly travels out to a remote rural area and gives lessons in Ugandan drumming and dancing as part of a flourishing Saturday morning music school. This recognition of the crucial importance of music in celebrating the cultural diversity which exists in South Africa has been recognised by government too.

An extract from a speech made by the Minister for Education in the Western Cape, Cameron Dugmore (2004), illustrates this point:

> "I am also pleased to announce that a tender will be called for to compile a first Western Cape Schools Songbook, as part of our 10-years of democracy celebrations. The songbook will reflect the rich diversity of all population groups in the province. It will create a home where the rich textures and fibre of our people are continuously celebrated. I will also seek to boost community institutions where the study and practice of contemporary and classical music, art and drama are encouraged. Our goal is to entrench arts and culture within our curriculum."

BUT WHAT'S DIFFERENT?

Rather than taking what some see as a narrowly subject-specific approach to learning in the arts as we have done in England, the curriculum in South Africa (www.polity.org.za/html/govdocs/policy/2002) has been divided into broad areas of study, called Learning Areas, and music is included in the Arts and Culture Learning Area. The learning outcomes for Arts and Culture are expressed in ways which are non-specific, but could be applied to all the arts; namely, creating, interpreting and presenting; reflecting; participating and collaborating; expressing and communicating (p6). There is an expectation that "learners will be assessed on all Learning Outcomes ... in all the art forms." (p9)

At the same time, the wider implications of the curriculum in South Africa are constantly borne in mind; educators are encouraged to think both in macro and micro terms at one and the same time. "All the Learning Area Statements try to create an awareness of the relationship between social justice, human rights, a healthy environment and inclusivity" (p2). This is a conscious attempt to develop pupils' understanding of the need for them to play an active part in the democratic process. "The framework is based on developmental skills acquisition, age appropriateness and national imperatives such as cultural diversity, human rights, environmental concerns, nation-building, heritage and power relations between global and local cultures" (p7). These issues are not just dealt with theoretically. Many practical examples are provided in order to give educators support in their planning and teaching. Take for example, one aspect of the Arts and Culture curriculum; that of requiring pupils to invent their own song about human rights issues. At Grade 7 (English equivalent Year 8), "The learner will be able to develop the skills and knowledge to create and present artworks that explore human rights in South Africa ... we know this when the learner composes music, songs or jingles about human rights issues or to accompany a performance or presentation about human rights." (p74)

From an English perspective, this could be seen as potentially controversial stuff; examining a human rights issue might provoke fierce debate in the classroom. But consider the average group of teenagers and their interests outside the school curriculum. Music teachers are used to coping with adolescent feelings running high in the context of the subject itself; they are all too familiar with having to manage and defuse situations where pupils have strong preferences in popular music and are very vocal about them! People of all social classes, cultures, and age groups have always used music as a medium and devised songs about perceived injustices of one form or another, be it a lover spurned, the lament of a soldier forced to fight battles far from home, or a wider issue in society at the time, such as the working conditions of miners or anti-slavery songs. Music and lyrics inspired by such topics is not just an area of interest for sociologists, but also legitimate material for musical study. There are worthwhile things to learn, not just about the lyrics of such songs but also about the stylistic choices made, any instrumentation used to accompany such songs, the musical structure, the shape of the melody and the vocal techniques employed to put across the desired message. Learners could be encouraged to write their own lyrics and song settings about a human rights issue of their choice; this would involve them in researching the area and discovering possible models for their own work. Models might include songs such as Bob Marley's *War*, a song advocating equal rights for all regardless of the colour of their skin, or more recently *Feed the World*, composed to support Bob Geldof's ongoing campaign against global inequalities.

SOME WAYS FORWARD

If we compare the curricula of the two countries, a range of contributory factors need to be taken into account, the chief factor being the recent past of South Africa and, therefore, the urgency of the project to develop democratic values in that country. These values permeate the whole school curriculum in all subject areas. By contrast, the English National Curriculum statement for Music appears to lack such joined-up thinking.

However the Music Programmes of study suggest: *"Music ... helps pupils to understand themselves and relate to others, forging important links between the home, school **and the wider world** ... encourages active involvement in different forms of ... music making, both individual and communal, developing a sense of group identity and togetherness ..."* (DfEE, 1999:14). The challenge for overworked teachers is that the relationships between citizenship education and the curriculum as a whole are not currently made sufficiently manifest. Because they were released before the introduction of the citizenship curriculum, neither the most recent National Curriculum programmes of study, which became statutory in 1999, or the QCA schemes of work for music, which were published in 2000 and are intended as optional supporting material, make explicit reference to curriculum links in the area of citizenship. No concrete examples are, therefore, currently available in government documents of how these ideals might be related to an actual Music lesson. One of the most common observations from students who have opted for the new citizenship pathway as part of their PGCE course in my institution is that schools have very good intentions about making links between subjects, but that making the links explicit in all subject areas is either non-existent or at a very early stage of development in their placement schools. Teachers are labouring under a sea of useful, but unconnected documentation; it is not surprising that a holistic approach is lacking.

I suggest that we can begin to make a start by making these links more explicit when training student teachers. We may already be modelling good practice in terms of a democratic approach in our lectures; for example, planning for opportunities for students to direct musical ensembles, to peer appraise work, to choose a topic for group compositions, ensuring that the tutor is not always in charge. We may already be reflecting cultural diversity through studying and experiencing at first hand a limited experience of world musics. We might also wish to adopt some specific examples from the South African Arts and Culture curriculum where the connections between the struggle for democracy, the need to acknowledge and celebrate cultural diversity within South Africa itself, and the recognition of the value that the arts can have in the continuing education for democratic participation, have been clearly made.

In addition to the suggestion made above about the human rights song, other aspects might be adapted and introduced in England; for example, on p16 of the Arts and Culture curriculum, Grade R (English equivalent Year 1) Participating and collaborating, we have *"The learner will be able to bring songs from home and share them with others."* Perhaps early years teachers in England who are not currently encouraging their children to do this might consider the idea? Recording songs sung by pupils from a range of different ethnic and cultural backgrounds could provide a rich resource to draw upon and help children to articulate and be proud of their different heritages. It would not be in conflict with the current National Curriculum for Music; it tunes in well with the statements in italics quoted above and is merely an expansion of *"developing knowledge skills and understanding through … a range of live and recorded music from different times and cultures."* (DfEE, 1999: paragraph 5) With reference to the citizenship curriculum for Key Stage One, it would also bring to life in an attractive and enjoyable way the idea of children preparing to take an active role as citizens; *"Pupils should be taught that they belong to various groups and communities, such family and school."* (DfEE, 1999: paragraph 2f)

Many schools these days encourage children to consider how they can contribute to an improvement in the environment; this idea from South Africa, making use of music as well as words, might be usefully applied in an English context:

From the Arts and Culture curriculum, Grade 5 (English equivalent Year 6) - (www.polity.org.za/html/govdocs/policy/2002)

> *"Expressing and Communicating: The learner will be able to use multiple resources to explore and communicate social, cultural and environmental issues through the arts… uses own compositions of poetry and song to draw attention to current social and environmental issues."* (p63)

A related issue is the use of everyday objects or 'junk' to make your own musical instrument. Apart from some folk traditions in England, this idea is rather foreign to us, although many music teachers are beginning to form their own 'junk' percussion ensembles which are very popular with pupils. Primary schools increasingly make their own musical instruments from rubbish such as plastic bags, bottles, cans, etc, as part of a study of environmental issues. In Africa, the idea of making one's own musical instrument is part of a long tradition, and this is included as part of the curriculum at Grade 4 (English equivalent of Year 5):

> *"The learner … makes in various tone colours, a simple wind instrument such as a Kazoo or Tshikona/Dinaka pipes, or percussion instruments such as shakers … creates and presents melodies using voice and found and natural instruments to demonstrate difference in pitch and note values."* (p44 Creating, interpreting and presenting)

The equal opportunities agenda is a familiar issue to teachers in England; much has been done to raise awareness of gender and cultural stereotyping. In Music, teachers are aware of the need to give equal access to opportunities for playing instruments (for example, drumkit to both boys and girls). In the South African curriculum, there is mention too of this issue. At Grade 7, for example, the learner *"Identifies and explains gender and/or cultural stereotyping in lyrics and in the use of instruments over time and in the present."* (p93)

CHALLENGES FOR PRACTITIONERS

The challenges in South Africa to music teacher educators, serving music teachers, and headteachers responsible for ensuring adequate coverage of the Arts and Culture curriculum come at a time of radical social change in every aspect of present-day life. Many of the challenges link back directly to the legacy of the apartheid regime.

Teacher training is undergoing radical change, with both tutors and students rethinking fundamental pedagogical models in order to adapt to outcomes-based education. Staffing for the arts in schools may be inappropriate for the new curriculum; for example, one school in a former coloured township in Durban has three people on the staff involved enthusiastically in teaching Music, but no-one prepared to take on the teaching of Art. In other schools it may be that some other permutation, also resulting in an unbalanced arts curriculum, is the case. This is not only limited to poorly resourced schools; for example, a well-run and respected high school in Durban that we visited has chosen to focus upon Drama in the later years, partly because they had great difficulty recruiting suitable staff.

A minority of white music teachers are reluctant to embrace the implications of the new curriculum. The combination of a multicultural and interdisciplinary approach is seen as threatening, because some teachers lack the expertise to deliver such a curriculum. There is a sense of not being able to cope with the broad spread of knowledge and skills required by the new curriculum, of having been trained for a high flying career of engagement with music in the Western classical tradition, and of having that expectation summarily removed. Under apartheid, for example, white class music teachers often worked in a situation where they not only taught whole class music, but also gave individual vocal and instrumental tuition to pupils. This is no longer an option and it is bitterly mourned by some. One white teacher now working in a former coloured township said during a workshop organised by the writer in Cape Town, *"I'm an opera singer; what do I know about African drumming?"* On the other hand, some white enthusiasts of classical music have decided that the changes in South Africa offer them a unique opportunity to share their love of Western classical music with all racial groups. In Pretoria, one teacher regularly gives workshops on music, movement, and story to young children in former African townships which introduce the children to famous pieces from the classical repertoire; she is much sought after and very popular.

Many African and coloured teachers seem to be embracing the new curriculum with enthusiasm; there are opportunities for professional development, even if relatively thin on the ground, and these seem to be taken up eagerly. At a workshop given in Cape Town integrating musical composition and performance, movement, art, and language in Arts and Culture lessons, African and coloured teachers took part with great gusto, eager to bring fresh ideas to their pupils and develop their ideas on integrated arts projects. Under the apartheid regime, the only aspect of music in which many schools in former African townships were involved in was singing. The new curriculum offers a much richer diet of engagement for all in the arts. The linking of the arts, music, dance, drama, visual arts, is a more 'African' approach. The result is an attempt to respect both traditions.

> *"Most African art forms and cultural practices are integrated … Western art forms are more inclined to remain discrete. This Learning Area Statement seeks to respect the integrity of each art form and to integrate them whenever possible, combining individual disciplines to create new forms of expression."* (www.polity.org.za/html/govdocs/policy/2002)

KEY POINTS

- Music can be a powerful means of valuing cultural diversity.

- Music is both a local and a global art. Developments in information and communication technology have increased opportunities for intercultural musical experiences.

- The South African curriculum makes explicit links with human rights issues, democracy in action and music education.

- The UK Music curriculum encourages the valuing of cultural diversity through music but there is a need for more explicit examples of how this might be done.

- Both the UK and South African have problems with funding a truly equitable music education programme for all.

- Governments in both the UK and South African recognise the value of music in promoting children's self esteem, ability to learn, and physical coordination skills.

SIGNPOSTS

- South African Arts and Culture Curriculum:
  www.polity.org.za/html/govdocs/ policy/2002/**curriculum**/part1 and
  www.polity.org.za/html/govdocs/ policy/2002/**curriculum**/part2

- Composing music – exploring sustainable development:
  http://www.smart-music-support.org.uk/profdev/articles.htm

- OXFAM teaching materials for Global Citizenship:
  http://www.oxfam.org.uk/coolplanet/index.htm

- Exploring Ubuntu through music: http://escalate.ac.uk/1760

POINTS FOR DISCUSSION

- Should we teach more songs in different languages in the UK to help pupils understand that linguistic diversity is the norm in many developing countries?

- Is there a role for links with the citizenship curriculum in terms of considering the role of protest songs, songs composed to disseminate issues, and the value of these activities in a healthy democracy?

- How much do we know about musical cultural diversity among our own pupils?

CONCLUSION:

HIV/AIDS - The greatest challenge of all currently facing South Africa. But what has it got to do with music?

I have chosen to write about this most important issue last of all. I hope it reflects something of the way in which HIV/AIDS is still dealt with in South African society. There is undoubtedly an unimaginably huge problem with HIV/AIDS in South Africa; it is much worse in some areas than others, but many people are still quite reluctant to talk about it, and this is understandable in many ways. It seems such a cruel irony that after years of struggle, freedom for all came coincidentally hand in hand with such a terrible scourge. Schools are using many ways to educate their pupils about possible infection. The invention of songs about HIV/AIDS, trying to pass on appropriate educational messages about disease prevention, is included and encouraged in the proposed content of the Music curriculum for pupils at Grade 11 (English equivalent Year 12), for example:

> "Identification and performance of suitable music that can reflect personal, social, or human rights issues such as HIV/AIDS songs, lamentations, rituals, songs about equal rights and ballads." (p31)

The important factor will be clarity and lack of ambiguity in the messages conveyed through song; who knows, the power of music may well contribute to an improvement in the present situation.

REFERENCES

Bunting, R. (2005) Muslim music and culture in the curriculum. *National Association of Music Educators' Magazine*. 16, pp13-15.

DfEE/QCA (1999) *The National Curriculum: Handbook(s) for Primary/Secondary Teachers in England.* London: DfEE/QCA.

DfES (2004) *Time for Standards - Transforming the School Workforce.* London: DfES.

Development Education Association (1998) *Training Teachers for tomorrow.* London: DEA. Downloadable from www.dea.org.uk

DfEE (1999) *All Our Futures: Creativity, Culture, and Education.* London: DfEE.

DfES (2004) *Every Child matters: Change for Children.* London: DfES.

Farrell, G. (1994) *Exploring the music of the world - Music of India.* London: Heinemann.

Farrell, G. (1990) *Indian music in education.* Cambridge: CUP.

Kwami, R. M. (2001) Music in and for a pluralist society *in* Philpott, C. and Plummeridge, C. (eds) (2001) *Issues in Music Teaching.* London: RoutledgeFalmer.

Levine, L. (2005) *The Drumcafe's Traditional Music of South Africa.* Jacana Media.

Stock, J. (2002) Concepts of World Music and their integration within western secondary music education *in* Spruce, G. (2002) (ed) *Aspects of Teaching Secondary Music.* London: RoutledgeFalmer.

SONG COLLECTIONS

Vermeulen, D. and van Aswegen, R. (1996) African Collage Class music activities, The Authors

Potgieter, H. (1998) (ed) *Lessons from South Africa.* Pretoria: University of Pretoria, Centre for Music Education.

Kutu, F. M. S. (1998) *Sina's songs.* Pretoria: University of Pretoria, Centre for Music Education.

CONCLUSION: LESSONS FROM UBUNTU

CLIVE HARBER AND JEFF SERF

Seeking Ubuntu was a project that sought to challenge a group of UK teacher educators to reflect on their own practice, and that of others, by exposing them to a range of experiences during a study visit to South Africa. This took place within an explicit framework which suggests that teacher education does not on the whole provide student teachers with a political analysis of education, does not equip teachers to handle controversial political issues (local or global) in the classroom and which does not use comparative or international examples to learn about the nature of education. In the life of any project there are events, incidents and comments that, at the time, register a permanent place in the collective memory and with hindsight give an indication of how well the project is progressing. One such moment came when Lebo Moletsane spoke to the group of the 'silences and taboos' that exist in South African education. If learners are to be prepared for life in a democratic society – and prepared they must be because democracy is not genetic, it is learned behaviour – such silences must be broken, such taboos addressed. There is nothing in our genes to programme us as democrats or dictators at birth. Education must have a clear idea of the sort of democratic person it hopes to cultivate and teachers must have clear strategies for the development of such people and, therefore, teacher educators need to be sure that their interactions with their students are conducive to education for democratic citizenship.

BREAKING THE SILENCE ABOUT THOSE TABOOS

Powerful forces are operating within the English education system that favour some sort of 'globalising of the curriculum'. However, we would argue that relatively little thought has been given to the characteristics of 'good' or 'effective' global education. For example, international links between learners, teachers, schools and other educational institutions are championed as valuable and desirable, but such links can not be divorced from the wider context within which they function. 'Educational tourism' (or even worse, 'educational voyeurism') by which teachers, pupils, principals and academics – in fact, anyone involved in the English education system – are jetted thousands of miles to experience education elsewhere in the world runs the risk of developing rather skewed views of what is to be seen and experienced. How can one begin to appreciate the demands placed on South African educators without an understanding of South African history? The country's constitution, with its clear statements on human rights and democratic participation, is a response to the injustices of Apartheid and is one of the most progressive in the world. The constitution permeates through educational policy and documentation, providing a clear vision of the democratic society that its people deserve, and whilst some South African educators express dissatisfaction about the implementation of education policies, there is strong admiration for the goals of those policies and the government's intentions.

If one needs a grasp of the macro-context of South Africa (i.e. how and why the state is 'behaving') to begin to understand its education system and the impact on the individuals involved within it, one also needs at least an awareness of the micro-context – how and why individuals are 'behaving'. The spectre of HIV/AIDS, traditional gender roles, masculinity and gender violence, inequitable access to resources and the professionalism of the professionals are all amongst the 'personal' factors that need to be considered and could all too easily be missed or avoided on a whistle-stop tour of South African schools.

The study group found that the project stimulated their thinking, not only about the South African context(s), but also about their own milieu. Each of the previous chapters contains what individuals saw as major points of learning, and these are presented as Key Points. Some of the Key Points relate to teaching methodology – for example, that teaching about HIV/AIDS is not easy or that teachers and schools can choose to be either passive or active in their approach to education for sustainable development. However, there is clear evidence that some student teachers are not being prepared to deal with controversial issues in their classrooms and this is a major omission because these issues cannot be kept outside the classroom. Neither are they being prepared to choose appropriate curriculum content or question externally imposed practices. South African educators criticise the manner in which they have been prepared to implement recent educational reforms, but the group concluded that the teachers they met felt they were part of the educational reform process and generally welcomed the changes. This, the group noted, contrasted with what they felt was a common opinion in England and Northern Ireland, that educational reform is imposed from above and thus is not received with such positive attitude.

Other Key Points consider organisational structures, and there would appear to be not a little evidence of the 'myth of the liberal college' referred to in the opening chapter. We have, we hope, come some way from the days when values were seen as having no place in education. However, we have yet to reach the situation, essential if education for democratic citizenship is to be truly effective, when the key values and aims underpinning the education system in general and individual schools in particular are open for debate, negotiation and clarification. Teachers need to be able to engage in such discussions with others involved in the education enterprise.

SO WHAT WAS LEARNED?

Seeking Ubuntu provided a structured experience for a group of teacher educators to reflect upon their own education systems and the role they play in preparing student teachers to engage in education for democratic citizenship. The group identified clear similarities between their own situation and that of fellow South African educators. For example, there can be little doubt that Moletsane's 'silences and taboos' exist in England and Northern Ireland.

In this book's preface, the following questions are posed as to what constitutes quality global learning:

- What do we want this 'global society' to look like?
- What does this 'work' involve?
- Who are our 'international partners'?
- What 'goals' do we have in common? Do we have some different, even conflicting, goals?
- Are we striving for global learning? Or should we be striving for Quality Global Learning? And if so, what are the characteristics of Quality Global Learning?

Seeking Ubuntu has, hopefully, begun to provide some possible answers. It provides significant evidence of the value of 'globalising the curriculum' that is offered to learners in schools and in our teacher training institutions; of the value of supporting educators to gain a broad and varied view of education; of the value of using a comparative experience to identify similarities and differences, explore options and different strategies; and of the value of providing educators with the space – physical, intellectual and temporal – in which to gain new knowledge, understanding and skills, explore what this enhancement means for their own practice.

Finally, what can *Seeking Ubuntu* offer in response to the last of the questions posed in the preface of this book? *What role does schooling and teacher education play in achieving these goals and providing Quality Global Learning?*

The need is for teacher educators who are able to see the need to challenge the myth of the liberal college and respond to that challenge; who will ensure that new teachers can contribute to the education of democratic citizens; who are able and willing to open the minds of their learners; and that resist the temptation to service a system that closes down the options of those in formal education.

Teacher educators need to address complex and controversial issues with their students so as to help build confidence so that they may, in turn, support learners in schools in exploring these issues. There are models of good practice, both in England and in South Africa, but there is an urgent need for effective CPD for teacher educators, teachers in school and teachers in training. Democratic practices are not incompatible with teacher education – in fact, they are essential if educators are to provide learners with the necessary knowledge, skills and experiences so they can become citizens in a democratic and increasingly globalised society.

Some challenges for thinking about global learning in the UK

❑ One of the more challenging ways of learning about our own society and its education system is to compare it with others. *How do we move away from the complacency of seeing ours as best?*

❑ Many teachers have not developed the skills to enable learners to engage with controversial issues. *What are the implications for ITE, CPD and creative curriculum planning?*

❑ Citizenship education is itself a contested area. *Do we offer learners the opportunity to understand this?*

❑ The potential purposes and goals of education are many … and are themselves controversial. *What purpose is proposed for global learning?*

❑ All education is political. *Is global learning fit for purpose?*

❑ Education can be <u>used</u> … for both 'good' and 'evil'. *How do we know what we are doing if we do not consider such questions?*

❑ What are our 'silences and taboos'? *Are there unquestioned assumptions about the 'global dimensions' agenda in England?*

ABBREVIATIONS

AIDS *Acquired Immuno-Deficiency Syndrome*

AQA *Assessment and Qualifications Alliance*

ART *Anti-retroviral treatment*

BNP *British National Party*

BSF *Building Schools for the Future*

CGE *Commission on Geographical Education*

CPD *Continuing Professional Development*

DCMS *Department for Culture, Media and Sport*

DEA *Development Education Association*

DfEE *Department for Education and Employment*

DfES *Department for Education and Skills*

DFID *Department for International Development*

ELRC *Education Labour Relations Council*

ESD *Education for Sustainable Development*

EU *European Union*

GA *Geographical Association*

GCE *General Certificate of Education*

GCSE *General Certificate of Secondary Education*

GEAR *Growth, Employment and Redistribution Strategy*

GTC *General Teaching Council*

GTIP *Geography Trainers' Induction Programme*

HE *Higher Education*

HEFCE *Higher Education Funding Council for England*

HIV *Human Immuno-deficiency Virus*

IGU *International Geographical Union*

INSET *In Service Training*

IQMS *Integrated Quality Management System*

ITE *Initial Teacher Education*

ITET *Initial Teacher Education Training*

KZN *KwaZulu Natal*

NCESS *National Committee on Education Support Services*

NCSNET *National Commission on Special Needs in Education and Training*

NFER *National Foundation for Educational Research*

NGO *Non-Governmental Organisation*

OBE *Outcomes Based Education*

OECD *Organisation for Economic Co-operation and Development*

Ofsted *Office for Standards in Education*

PESS *Physical Education and School Sport*

PESSCL *Physical Education, School Sport and Club Link*

PGCE *Post Graduate Certificate in Education*

PHSE *Personal, Health and Social Education*

PISA *Programme for International Student Assessment*

PSA *Public Service Agreement*

QCA *Qualifications and Curriculum Authority*

QTS *Qualified Teacher Status*

RSA *Royal Society for the Encouragement of Arts*

SATs *Standard Assessment Tests*

SEN *Special Educational Needs*

SENDA *Special Education Needs and Disability Act*

TES *Times Educational Supplement*

Tide~ *Teachers in Development Education*

UNAIDS *Joint United Nations Programme on HIV/ AIDS*

UNGASS *UN General Assembly Special Session*

YST *Youth Sport Trust*

COMPARATIVE EDUCATION AND QUALITY GLOBAL LEARNING:

ENGAGING WITH CONTROVERSIAL ISSUES IN SOUTH AFRICA AND THE UK

Edited by Clive Harber, Jeff Serf and Scott Sinclair

Authors

Liz Bartley, Sue Bermingham, Linda Clarke, Clive Harber, Jenny Hughes, Jackie Lambe, Helen Miles, Doreen Oakley, Jeff Serf, Karen Teasdale, Richard Woolley

Published by and available from: **Tide~ global learning**
Millennium Point
Curzon Street
Birmingham, B4 7XG

ISBN: 978-0-948838-39-2

FOREWORD

This book is one of the outcomes of *Seeking Ubuntu*, a Tide~ project that involved a group of UK teacher educators in a study visit to South Africa. Comparative study supported them in reflecting on their own, as well as South African, educational practice.

It offers some insights into that experience featuring the authors' analyses of education in both South Africa and the United Kingdom and about how they used the experience to evaluate their everyday practice as teacher educators.

The project built on earlier Tide~ work focusing on South Africa that led to:

- *Towards Ubuntu – critical teacher education for democratic citizenship in South Africa and England*

- *Exploring Ubuntu – education & development: an introduction to theories and debates*

These projects have strengthened our disposition that the idea of Ubuntu is fundamental to a positive vision of future society … local and global. Ubuntu is a Zulu concept that translates approximately to human dignity. Such dignity is also core to thinking about quality global learning and the role schools have in shaping a future that builds strong democratic citizenship and a society that responds positively to the challenges of its global dynamic.

Tide~ global learning is in many ways about seeking Ubuntu. This book highlights many perspectives that need to be part of an international debate about the role of education to build a better future built on the commonality of our global experiences. The website www.tidegloballearning.net features other work from Tide~ Ubuntu projects.

The final chapter concludes with challenges for thinking about global learning in the UK. [page 107]. We are reminded that *education can be used for 'good' or 'evil'*. It is not apolitical, nor uncontested. We are asked … how do we know what we are doing if we do not consider questions about our own assumptions?

Tide~ global learning seeks to offer the 'space' for practitioners to work together on such issues, to develop practical outcomes and to build a common understanding of what quality might look like in terms of global learning … and meeting the needs of learners growing up in an increasingly globalised society.

Scott Sinclair
Director, Tide~ global learning